W9-AHM-422

The SEEDS *of* innovation

Cultivating the Synergy That Fosters New Ideas

Elaine Dundon

AMACOM
American Management Association
New York • Atlanta • Brussels • Buenos Aires • Chicago • London • Mexico City
San Francisco • Shanghai • Tokyo • Toronto • Washington, D.C.

Special discounts on bulk quantities of AMACOM books are available to corporations, professional associations, and other organizations. For details, contact Special Sales Department, AMACOM, a division of American Management Association, 1601 Broadway, New York, NY 10019.
Tel: 212-903-8316. Fax: 212-903-8083.
E-mail: specialsls@amanet.org
Website: www.amacombooks.org/go/specialsales
To view all AMACOM titles go to: www.amacombooks.org

Library of Congress Cataloging-in-Publication Data

Dundon, Elaine, 1959–
The seeds of innovation: cultivating the synergy that fosters new ideas / Elaine Dundon.
p. cm.
Includes bibliiographical references and index.
ISBN-10: 0-8144-7146-3
ISBN-13: 978-0-8144-7146-3
1. Technological innovations—Management. 2. New products.
3. Creative thinking. I. Title.

HD45 D86 2002
658.4'063—dc21 *2002016418*

Printing number

10 9 8

Dedication

This book is dedicated to my wonderful husband, Alex, who gave me the push I needed to leave the safety of the ground and fly toward my dreams. For this, I will be forever grateful.

CONTENTS

Appendices

PREFACE

Over the last few years, I have witnessed a growing interest in the field of Innovation Management. Now more than ever, in an era of economic uncertainty, constrained resources, and increased global competition, more and more organizations are turning to Innovation Management as a source of new solutions and renewed inspiration.

At the same time, however, I have witnessed a growing frustration surrounding the lack of clarity as to what Innovation Management is all about. I see many organizations declaring innovation as an objective but then failing to follow up with any concrete action steps or support. Perhaps they are just hoping that someone, somehow, will find *the* breakthrough idea their organization needs to dramatically improve revenue or cut costs. In most cases, I have also found that management, as well as employees, limits its view of innovation to creative thinking. Creativity is certainly a part of innovation, but only a part. Innovation is so much more.

Unlike any other book in the marketplace, this book combines the three powerful components, or "seeds," of innovation—*creative thinking, strategic thinking,* and *transformational thinking* (the "human dimension" of innovation)—into one powerful resource. Combining the learning from all three of these areas creates the synergy needed to foster new ideas—whether it is at the individual, team, or organization level.

In this book, you will learn:

- Why innovation isn't just for "right-brain creative thinkers."

- That innovation applies to more than just "new products" and "new technology."

- That Evolutionary Innovation (small but different ideas) is as valuable as, if not more valuable than, Revolutionary Innovation (radically different ideas).

- Why current approaches to brainstorming are actually limiting your innovative thinking abilities—and specific ways to overcome these limitations.

- Why "seeing the big picture" and "looking to the future" are fundamental to spotting opportunities before everyone else does.

- Where and how to look for creative ideas, using creative-thinking tools that you can apply immediately to dramatically increase not only the *quantity* of ideas but the *quality* of your ideas as well.

- How to turn your creative ideas into high-value, *strategic ideas* using the "Nine Extraordinary Strategies."

- How to prepare and *present* your idea to maximize its appeal and double your chances of "closing the sale."

- How to maximize your team's *collaborative innovation* output using the principles of the "Innovation Systems Architecture®" model. Find out how to strengthen your team's capacity for innovation and ensure that your team has more Innovation Supporters than Innovation Killers!

The Seeds of Innovation presents a *disciplined, yet practical* approach to innovation based on the very successful Innovation Management course at the University of Toronto, the first of its kind in North America. Many of the powerful insights and easy-to-use techniques presented in this book have been field-tested with top corporations and government agencies around the world, including Aliant, AstraZeneca, Four Seasons Hotels and Resorts, Hewlett-Packard, Frito-Lay, Kraft Foods, Molson Breweries, Oracle, Procter & Gamble, and the USDA Forest Service.

I specifically chose examples that are not industry-sector-specific to prove that all industries can be innovative. It is important to look for innovative ideas outside your own industry sector and bring these ideas into your own sector before your competition does. This enables you to lead, not follow, your competition.

The Innovation Management models, processes, and innovative-thinking tools presented in this book have been designed to help you break down the barriers of conventional thinking, to challenge assumptions about "the way we do things around here," and to identify ideas that will add value, not only on an individual basis, but also for the entire organization.

My philosophy is that the best ideas are usually the simplest. For this reason, I have taken some very complex concepts and simplified them so that they are easier to understand and apply. I do urge you to explore in more depth those areas that particularly interest you. The Recommended Reading List can help jump-start your additional research.

So stop wasting valuable time and money on unfocused innovation efforts. Dramatically enhance your ability to identify, develop, sell, and implement your innovative ideas using the proven techniques presented in *The Seeds of Innovation*. The easy-to-understand and easy-to-apply approach to innovation presented in this book is a truly unique resource that will help you and your team bring a higher level of innovation to your organization as well as to the marketplace.

ACKNOWLEDGMENTS

Writing a book is like growing a garden. One cannot expect to plant a seed and have a full-grown flower the next day. I certainly could not have completed this book without the creative energies, strategic guidance, personal support, and above all, the patience of many along the way.

First, I owe a great deal to my wonderful husband, Alex, who always believes in me and continually inspires me to persevere along my journey of self-discovery. He is a marvelous muse. The creative spirits and passions of my mother and her brother, Uncle Louie, are alive on many of the pages of this book. They taught me so much about respecting others for the greater good.

I would like to thank my father, my teachers, and my mentors, who taught me along my life's journey and instilled in me the belief that there is always more than one right way to do something. I want to thank my students, whose fresh perspectives and incessant energy pushed me to think in new ways. And I certainly owe a great deal to my many clients, who shared their insights and lessons so that I might learn as well as teach.

The team at AMACOM provided much-needed guidance throughout this creative journey. I would like to thank Ellen Kadin, senior acquisitions editor, who made the pivotal decision to proceed with this book; Christina McLaughlin, developmental editor, who readily shared her time and her extraordinary ideas while guiding the development of this manuscript; Cathleen Ouderkirk, creative director, whose creative talent shines through on the book jacket; and Jim Bessent and the rest of the editing and production team who nurtured *The Seeds of Innovation* along its journey.

The SEEDS *of* innovation

Introduction to Innovation Management

"Our team holds lots of brainstorming sessions and we have plenty of creative ideas. We just don't do anything with them!"

"Our innovative ideas come from the same people all the time. The others just sit back and wait for these people to discover the next big idea."

"We're spinning our wheels faster and faster, but we don't seem to be making any progress in the marketplace."

Do these comments sound familiar? Why is it that some individuals, teams, or organizations seem to be able to push the boundaries of what is possible today in search of a better tomorrow while others are not? How are Nelson Mandela (the former president of South Africa),

Michael Dell (Dell Computer Corporation), Sir Richard Branson (Virgin Group), Anita Roddick (The Body Shop), Jesse Ventura (governor of Minnesota), Dee Hock (VISA), Bill Gates (Microsoft Corporation), and many other lesser-known people able to see a new perspective in order to rewrite "the way things are supposed to be done"? How are organizations such as Charles Schwab & Co., Four Seasons Hotels and Resorts, Hewlett-Packard, Southwest Airlines, Starbucks, Roots, and Wal-Mart able to change the rules of the game to gain leadership in their respective market segments?

For these organizations, innovation is a priority. Each of them strives to create an "innovation-centric culture" where everyone is encouraged to take an active role in innovation, where new ideas and approaches are welcome, where the power of technology and branding are well understood, and where attention is focused both on pleasing today's customer and on planning for tomorrow's customer. The leaders of these organizations know that they must "drive with their high beams on" to analyze the marketplace and choose a distinctly better path for the future. And once this path has been chosen, they galvanize their teams to move quickly.

Unfortunately, there are other organizations that are traveling down the same highways without their headlights on. Many organizations that were once leaders in their field are now struggling to stay afloat. Their leaders are so busy managing the current businesses that they fail to look up and realize that the marketplace has changed. They fail to see the need for innovation.

The Need for Innovation

The world has always needed innovation. From the invention of the wheel to the invention of the car, the telephone, the television, and the Internet, we have profited from manifestations of the innovative spirit. So what makes the need for innovation different today?

We are in the midst of a significant transition, largely as the result of three main factors: technology, the expanding world, and more demanding customers.

1. ***Technology.*** Even the most stable industries and the strongest brands can be blown to bits by the new information technology. "The glue that holds today's value chains and supply chains together . . . is melting."[1] Technology is forcing every organization to rethink its business models and organizational designs as it contributes to the rebalancing of power in the marketplace. First place is no longer guaranteed to those organizations that have financial resources and size on their side. Smaller organizations that are fast and flexible can now outmaneuver the traditional "large cats" by employing new technology that enables them to deliver goods and services to their customers at a faster pace and lower cost. The unfortunate aspect of technology is the harsh reality that machines can replace people. Automatic banking machines have replaced tellers. Internet sites have replaced sales personnel. Photo radar has replaced police patrols. Technology allows customers to do-it-themselves, with little or no need for service personnel. On the one hand, an organization must keep pace with new technology in order to remain competitive, while on the other hand, individuals must stay one step ahead of this new technology so that they are not replaced by the very thing they are recommending!

2. *The Expanding World*. The Internet, international air travel, CNN, and low-cost long-distance telephone rates are just a few examples of how the entire world is becoming more accessible. Everyone now has more buying options; for example, a company no longer has to hire a consultant who lives nearby; with online learning, a student no longer has to choose the closest university. But as boundaries come down, the level of competition goes up. More and more competitors are fighting for the same dollar. Searching for new sources of revenue, companies are expanding beyond their classic definition of "the business we are in." Not only are companies expanding their businesses into new market segments, they are also expanding their businesses into new geographic territories. It's no longer enough just to look at the competitor down the street. Now competitors from around the world, from India, Germany, and Brazil, as well as from other countries whose names are rarely heard, need to be considered.

The more competition there is, the more overloaded with products and services the world becomes. How do consumers choose the best computer to buy when they are offered thousands of options either locally or on the Internet? The ability to differentiate these products and services from each other is becoming a tougher and tougher challenge.

3. ***More Demanding Customers.*** Customers, sensing that they have more choice and more buying power, are becoming more and more demanding. Perhaps Burger King should be blamed for starting the "have it your way" movement. Customers want it their way and they want it now! Companies need to balance the customers' need for customization with their own operational need to pump out mass volume in order to realize higher margins.

Innovative Organizations Are More Profitable

In addition to responding to technology, the expanding world, and more demanding customers, adopting a more innovative approach has additional benefits. According to the 1999 Global Growth and Innovation Study conducted by PricewaterhouseCoopers, "innovation has been confirmed as a lever of growth and value creation." [2] A positive innovation image:

- Attracts shareholders and can add value to the organization's stock price. The stock market is based on present and future value predictions for a company. That's why Amazon.com could record minimal profit yet still have a high stock valuation.

- Attracts new employees. An innovative image helps your recruitment efforts, especially in this tight labor market where talent is becoming a scarce commodity.

- Retains current employees. Most employees want to work for a progressive company that is known for innovation and where they feel their contribution is valued.

Most managers understand the critical importance of innovation as a competitive advantage. They understand the need for organizations to do a much better job at innovation-management-related activities, including building their capacity in innovation processes and aligning innovation efforts with strategic intent. According to a recent Arthur D. Little survey of 700 organizations world-wide, 84 percent of business leaders agreed that innovation is a more critical success factor than it was five years ago, but only 25 percent of these business leaders were pleased with their current performance in innovation.[3]

Expand Your Own Definition of Innovation

Many organizations are beginning to realize that what got them to where they are today might not get them through the next five years. According to Peter Drucker, "every organization—not just business—needs one core competence–innovation."[4] It only seems appropriate that, in times of economic challenge, global competition, and an overabundance of similar products and services, leaders would turn to innovation as the new corporate mantra. Unfortunately, the concept of innovation has been so widely used and misused that many people are now confused as to what it really is.

A good starting point is to develop a common understanding and definition of what the term *innovation* means to you and the members of your team and organization. Take time to discuss and agree upon your own definition.

Based on applied research, interviews with executives and managers, as well as practical experience working with many international companies and other organizations, my associates and I have developed a common definition of innovation, which combines four key components:

1. ***Creativity***—the discovery of a *new idea.*

2. ***Strategy***—determining whether it is a new and *useful* idea.

3. ***Implementation***—putting this new and useful idea into *action.* It is in the area of implementation that many great creative and potentially innovative ideas become blocked and never have a chance to deliver value to an organization. Managers are often afraid to take the risk on new ideas and throw a lot of hurdles up to prevent change. In addition, the ideas are often not presented or packaged in the right way to enable people to understand their potential.

4. ***Profitability***—maximizing the *added value* from the implementation of this new and useful idea. The concept of profit can manifest itself in many ways, such as a financial gain, an improvement in employee morale or retention, or an increase in the contribution to society. Profitable implementation also considers the resources needed to develop and implement the new idea. Some organizations spend too much launching the new idea and soon find that they cannot sustain the spending level. Other companies miscalculate the amount of time and effort the launch may involve, taking away from managing the rest of the portfolio. Still other companies overestimate the potential of an idea or business concept that is actually quite weak. The recent round of failures of technology companies is evidence of this illusion.

The definition of *innovation* is "the profitable implementation of strategic creativity." This goes beyond simply referring to the act of creativity or the identification of new ideas. Use this definition as food for thought in developing your own definition of innovation.

What Innovation Is Not!

It might be helpful for you and your team to discuss how the concept of innovation can be integrated within your own organization. The following list will help broaden your view of the concept of innovation.

- ***Innovation is not just "new technology."*** Although the term innovation has been linked closely with technology, it can be viewed in a much broader context. For example, innovation can relate to packaging, customer delivery services, social programs, and many other things.

- ***Innovation is not sector-specific.*** Many innovative organizations operate outside the technology and manufacturing sectors. There are many examples of innovations in the pharmaceutical, entertainment, airline, and public service sectors.

- ***Innovation is not just for the research and development department.*** Although this department has typically been associated with innovation due to its involvement in the front-end or early stages of identifying a new product or service, innovation can occur at all stages of the planning process and in all four corners of the organization. As the complexities of organizational life increase, leaders need *all* employees to participate in finding new ways to strengthen the organization. Depriving employees outside the research and development department of the ability to participate in the innovation program deprives the organization of valuable resources.

- ***Innovation is not isolated to special teams or "skunkworks."*** Innovation can be applied to the day-to-day activities of all departments and not specifically reserved for special projects assigned to special teams that are hidden away in remote locations.

- ***Innovation is not a creative playroom.*** Creating the right conditions for innovation goes far beyond providing a special room with comfortable chairs, toys, and magazines. The right environment has more to do with creating a supportive and open culture, designing streamlined process networks, allocating resources to develop and implement new ideas, providing targeted training to enable team members to build their innovative-thinking skills, and rewarding innovative efforts.

- ***Innovation is not a one-off event.*** Although we typically see a surge of innovative thinking during the month set aside for developing next year's plan, innovation should be viewed as a year-round activity. The overall goal of Innovation Management is to create the capacity for sustained innovation.

- ***Innovation is not just creativity training.*** Although creative-thinking skills are important, strategic skills—the ability to develop these creative ideas into ones that can bring added value to the organization—and transformational skills—the ability to present and gain acceptance for the implementation of these new ideas—are just as important.

- ***Innovation is not just applicable to new products.*** Innovation can be applied to many areas of the organization including: 1) new products, services, or programs; 2) existing products, services, or programs; 3) processes an organization uses to plan and manage its activities; and 4) totally new business models or concepts.

There Is More Than One Application for Innovation

While innovation related to *new products and services* tends to receive the most attention, innovation focused on *existing products or services* should not be overlooked. Small improvements on existing products may deliver big returns. For example, securing a new distribution channel, repositioning a current service to attract a new group of customers, or improving the quality of the current product can often deliver higher returns than launching a new initiative from scratch. Often simply shifting the emphasis from one area of the portfolio to another or focusing on a forgotten program can deliver the same, if not better, results than adding a new product.

Adding a service to a product, such as teaching the customer how to use the product, or customizing the product for a certain customer or customer group, can also add value. Conversely, adding a product to a service, such as distributing free books at a seminar or distributing a book on Italy to diners at an Italian restaurant, could also represent innovative ways to add value to a service.

While introducing new products and services may be exciting in some circumstances, it might be wise to just leave the product alone. Coca-Cola discovered this the hard way when it replaced its Coke product with New Coke. The only problem was that consumers didn't see anything wrong with the traditional Coke formula and therefore rebelled against the launch of New Coke.

It might be wiser to focus on the third area of innovation: the processes an organization uses to plan and manage its activities. Innovation can be applied to internal processes like those used to complete such tasks as budgeting, cross-functional planning, human-resource performance reviews, and production planning. Innovation can also be applied to the external processes used to interact with external stakeholders, such as planning raw-material deliveries with suppliers, ensuring on-time delivery to customers, or gaining regulatory approval from a government agency. With the oversupplied marketplace, the basis of competition is shifting from product-based competition to process-based competition. As more and more products and services are being offered to the consumer with little or no differentiation, organizations are looking for ways to distinguish between these products and services. While some people do not see Dell computers as superior to those offered by the competition, they must agree that Dell Computer Corporation is an innovative organization. Michael Dell found a brilliant way to differentiate his product by offering a better selling process which included order fulfillment through 1-800 phone technology and the Internet, built-to-order computers, and direct-to-home delivery. It was process innovation, not product innovation, that helped position Dell as a leader in personal computer sales.

Innovation can also refer to the total business model or concept the organization is using. Often organizations are so tied to their current business models that they find it difficult to rethink their entire model. Many organizations are following business models that are outdated. University teaching is one example of a sector facing new challenges, such as online learning, the inability to attract qualified professors in specialized fields, and a more demanding student population. Unfortunately, some universities are trying very hard to hold on to their historical business models. Perhaps creating new services, forging new alliances, and outsourcing nonessential elements of the service could represent a better business model.

In light of the oversupplied economy, you should devote some effort to evaluating the strength and relevance of your current business model.

Determine What Type of Innovation You Want

What were the top three innovations your team or organization introduced to the marketplace in the last twelve months? Were these innovations 1) small, internally focused productivity improvements; 2) incremental changes in the marketplace; or 3) radically new changes in the marketplace? In other words, were they Efficiency, Evolutionary, or Revolutionary Innovation activities? Ask yourself in which of these three categories your team is spending most of its effort.

An easy-to-understand illustration of the range of possible approaches for innovation is *The Innovation Value Continuum* shown below:

Efficiency Innovation	**Evolutionary Innovation**	**Revolutionary Innovation**

Efficiency Innovation focuses on identifying new ideas for improving what already exists. This approach requires minimal investment since the team is building on the past and only looking for small changes in what is already being done. These innovations are lower-impact improvements or adaptations of an organization's products, services, programs, or processes. The strategy for Efficiency Innovations is usually to cut costs, reduce cycle time, improve quality, offset a competitor's move, or attract new customers. Typically, only small gains are realized. Examples of Efficiency Innovations are

- Extending the hours of service at a McDonald's restaurant to 24 hours;
- Enabling the same machinery to work faster or with greater accuracy;
- Developing a standardized format for reporting monthly activities by department or function.

Some view the pursuit of efficiency as opposite to thc pursuit of innovation. However, if the definition of innovation is the profitable implementation of strategic creativity (new and useful ideas), then even small ideas for cost savings or productivity programs should be considered part of the Innovation Value Continuum. We have seen many companies, such as the Japanese manufacturers Nissan, Sony, and NEC, benefit from reworking what already exists.

Pursuing Efficiency Innovation is the optimal route in some cases. Sometimes there is so much chaos and misalignment within an organization that stopping for a while to get the fundamentals right is the smartest thing to do. Instead of introducing new products or services on top of a weak infrastructure, it might be wise to take a little time to agree to the portfolio priorities: which products to promote, which to hold, and which to discontinue. It is also wise to take time to improve the current work processes. Retrenching for a while can help focus and strengthen the organization to return to fight the next battle. Reducing costs may also create a cost advantage that can shield the organization from new competition and provide enough funds to invest in future innovative ideas.

In other circumstances though, pursuing Efficiency Innovation is not the optimal route. Cost-savings programs may appear to be a quick route to higher profits but, in actuality, may be costing more than the organization anticipated. These initiatives may have a negative effect on the quality of your customer offerings as well as on the psyche of your employees. Launching multiple line extensions may lead to operation inefficiencies, customer confusion, and ineffective allocation of resources. Importantly, these activities may be taking the focus away from opportunities that could deliver better returns and have a higher impact on the future health of the organization.

While Efficiency Innovation focuses on identifying ideas to improve what already exists, **Evolutionary Innovation** focuses on identifying ideas that represent something "distinctly new and better." An example of an Evolutionary Innovation is the introduction of automatic banking machines that changed the way banks viewed their staffing needs and shifted banking habits from set hours to banking at any hour.

Evolutionary Innovation requires the team to look more broadly than Total Quality Management (TQM) and cost-savings initiatives to see the bigger picture of what is really needed in the organization and marketplace. Instead of duplicating what already exists, the team must look for new ways to bring value to the organization and the customer. Evolutionary Innovations include "distinctly new and better" products and services or "distinctly new and better" processes, which can change the way customers relate to the organization or the way work is processed within the organization.

Efficiency Innovation and Evolutionary Innovation operate within the existing structure of the organization and marketplace, whereas **Revolutionary Innovation** focuses on radically new and better ideas that may, in fact, dismantle the existing structure of the organization and marketplace. For example, McDonald's approach to fast food changed the restaurant business. Dell Computer Corporation's direct-to-consumer sales strategy changed the computer industry. Disney's unique characters and interactive theme parks changed the entertainment business. Napster and MP3 technology jolted the music industry. Bluetooth convergence technology will change the technology industry, and the Internet changed and will continue to change all industry sectors.

In reality, only a very few organizations and only a very few individuals are actually working on anything revolutionary. In fact, the majority of effort is focused not on Revolutionary Innovation or even Evolutionary Innovation but on Efficiency Innovation. In times of economic uncertainty, people become more cautious and slip back into the efficiency mode in an attempt to control what is perceived to be the most controllable part of the business—the cost structure. Some may find it more comforting to work on the smaller issues facing the team, delaying the larger issues for another time. Most people like to work on what they know. Still others may not see the need for anything new and better.

The problem arises when organizations are spending too much time tinkering with small, low-impact innovations instead of rallying their teams around the potential to do something extraordinary in the marketplace. Tinkering is like painting the car when the engine is weak. Canadian Airlines was busy repainting its fleet of airplanes with an image of the Canadian goose while its passenger loads were weak. Repainting a plane will not result in a significant increase in passenger travel and, in turn, increased profitability.

Although Efficiency Innovation may be too limiting, Revolutionary Innovation, which is at the other end of the continuum, may be too disruptive. If the marketplace and organization are not ready for the revolutionary idea, there will be a tremendous amount of resistance to change that could sabotage the acceptance of the new idea. Simply having a revolutionary idea or strategy does not, in any small measure, guarantee success with the human side of innovation!

If a focus on Efficiency Innovation is too limiting and a focus on Revolutionary Innovation too disruptive, a focus on Evolutionary Innovation may be just right! Many of the great companies in the last twenty years succeeded by implementing new, evolutionary ideas on a continual basis. Many football games have been won by the quarterback's opting for the ground game with continual yardage gains instead of throwing long-distance touchdowns. Continual focus on "evolutionary ideas" may be the optimal approach for your team.

What is important is to be honest about the type of innovation you and your team really want. Many leaders send out conflicting signals. They ask for Revolutionary Innovation ideas only to criticize them for fear of the unknown once they are presented. The only ideas such leaders will support are very small-impact efficiency ideas. It is very important at the beginning of any project to discuss the type of innovation the team is expecting. What type of innovation is doable in light of the available resources and the core competencies and culture of the team and organization?

Evolutionary Innovations can play a significant role in building the innovation momentum for an organization. Like a snowball gaining size and power as it rolls down the hill, an organization gains power as more and more employees adopt an innovative attitude and succeed in finding distinctly new and better ideas.

The Seeds of Innovation

Innovation is easier said than done. In order to move along the Innovation Value Continuum, it is important to develop innovative-thinking skills. As every good farmer knows, you can't expect new plants to sprout from old seeds. It takes the seeds of creative thinking, strategic thinking, and transformational thinking to cultivate the synergy that fosters new ideas.

The *seeds of creative thinking* include believing in creativity, being curious, and discovering new connections. Once the creative idea has been identified, it must be developed into a strategic idea so that it can bring value to the organization and the marketplace.

The *seeds of strategic thinking* include seeing the BIG Picture, understanding the present but looking to the future, and doing the extraordinary.

The *seeds of transformational thinking* involve the human side of innovation and include seeking greater awareness in dealing with the resistance to change, building the collaborative networks needed to support new ideas, developing courage and igniting passion, and, above all, taking action.

Just before we move on to looking at the seeds of creative thinking, it is important to introduce an innovation planning process that will be referenced throughout this book.

The Nine-Step Innovation Process

Some organizations have designed and implemented specific innovation processes for developing new products or guiding project management. While these processes might be valuable to the specific team, they are not necessarily applicable to innovation work, nor are they applicable to all employees across the organization. What is needed is a systematic process that can guide the innovative efforts in any department, organization, or industry sector, whether they are corporate, government, or non-profit. What is needed is a framework or process that can guide innovation activities from start to finish.

My Nine-Step Innovation Process has been designed to be applicable for most projects across departments in any industry sector. The work required can be performed by individuals or cross-functional teams at any step in the process. The steps of the process will be discussed in various chapters throughout this book. For your reference, a diagram of the complete process is provided in Appendix A.

As an introduction, the three key stages of the process are:

1. *Understanding*. It is critical to understand what the problem really is before you go off and start to solve it. The first stage of the overall process, *Understanding,* involves gathering background information, formulating potential problem statements from multiple perspectives, and determining the range of potential solutions by setting the Innovation Goalposts.

2. *Imagination*. The second stage involves gathering as many stimuli as possible in order to maximize the probability of making new connections. With the stimuli and an active imagination, participants are able to find new insights. From these insights, new ideas will be identified.

3. *Action*. The third stage involves building the ideas into full business concepts and then into business plans. These plans are presented in accordance with the strategic Innovation Goalposts, making acceptance more realistic and more plausible. From here, the ideas are implemented and reviewed for shared learning.

Although the nine steps are presented in a linear fashion in the process, it is important to note that the value in using the process is to guide the exploration and discussion of innovation, not to provide a rigid prescription for innovation planning. You and your team are encouraged to loop back to previous steps if necessary at any point in the process.

PART 1

The SEEDS *of* creative thinking

CHAPTER 1

Believe in Creativity

Without creativity, there is no innovation. As every good gardener knows, you can't rely on the same old flowers season after season. They die. New seeds are needed to rejuvenate the garden and stimulate growth.

Field experience has shown that roughly half of the people surveyed believe they have skills in creativity while the other half are filled with doubts about their creative abilities. One of the fundamental principles of Innovation Management is "Believe in Creativity." As many great psychologists will tell you, "If you think you can, you can and if you think you can't, you can't!"

Let's take a look at this belief in creativity.

Believe That *Everyone* Is Creative

Why do some individuals have a greater ability to discover new and often amazing ideas than others? Why are some, like Jerry Seinfeld, able to make connections between things that make people laugh and think, "Why didn't I think of that?" Are these people born with this creative ability, or is it gained through supportive parents, mentors, or other environmental factors? Is creativity a mystery, an untouchable skill with which only a few are blessed?

Many view creativity as an integral part of the DNA with which everyone is born. Others view creativity as a "lucky break," usually reserved for those who have a natural talent for creative expression, like Shakespeare, Van Gogh, da Vinci, or Disney. Those are the special ones, the gifted ones, the crazy ones. These gifted ones supposedly gravitate to "creative" fields like advertising and the arts, but certainly not to fields like finance or medicine. Why is it that an advertising person who discovers a new idea to communicate with potential customers is called "creative," but a purchasing manager who discovers a new idea to source raw materials at a cheaper rate, or a human resources manager who discovers a new idea to recruit students via the Internet, is not? Is creative thinking the domain of only a few?

No. If the definition of creativity is "the discovery of a new connection," then *everyone* has the ability to be creative. Everyone has the ability to connect one idea with another, to find an idea in another department, organization, or industry, and connect it with another to solve the challenge at hand. Artistic creativity is only one form of creativity. There are many other forms or avenues of creative expression, such as finding a new idea to better serve a customer, discovering a new recipe using only the ingredients in the refrigerator, or trying a new route to and from work.

Figure 1-1 is a list of several traits commonly associated with creative thinkers. Everyone possesses some of these creative-thinking traits. Identify *your* creative traits.

Believe in Your Own Unique Creative-Thinking Talents

Were you once creative, but now suppress your creativity in an effort to conform? Or have you lost faith in your creative ability because someone, somewhere in your past, planted the seeds of self-doubt about your creative ability? The most important factor in creative thinking is a person's own belief in his creative ability. A leader cannot just ask people to be creative. They must first believe that they are.

Figure 1-1. Traits of the creative thinker.

Willing to challenge the status quo	Enjoys complexity
Curious	Has many interests
Adventurous	Enjoys a challenge
Imaginative	Intuitive
Able to make connections	Able to see new possibilities
Observant	Motivated
Flexible	Collaborative
Reflective	Analytical
Playful	Patient
Tolerates being in the unknown	Persistent
Continuously learning	

Not everyone is creative in the same way. Everyone has different preferences and talents for creativity in different areas of their life. For example, Bill Gates may be a creative thinker in the computer field but might not be as creatively inclined with gardening. Wayne Gretsky might be a creative thinker when it comes to hockey and reading the relationships between players on the ice, but he might not be as creative when it comes to composing short stories. Albert Einstein might have been a great creative thinker when it came to mathematics, but he might not have been as creative as an athlete. You might be very creative in one area of your life and less so in another.

There are many situations in everyday life in which an individual's creative-thinking talent is needed. Creative ideas are needed when faced with the challenge of finding a birthday gift, figuring out a new route to work when the regular route is under construction, or locating a long-lost classmate. The fundamental skills of creative thinking in these situations can be transferred to creative problem-solving in a work setting. If you have shown your creative-thinking abilities in one area of your life, what is stopping you from transferring these same skills to other areas of your life, including your work?

Try these creative-thinking exercises:

- Your budget has been cut in half. What would you do?
- Your budget has doubled. What would you do?

- Identify a new name for a peanut-butter chocolate bar.
- Name five new uses for "bubblewrap."
- You have just won a million dollars. What would you do? (This may be the easiest of the five creative-thinking exercises!)

Assessment Tools

People often turn to assessment tools or profiles to give them greater insight into their creative-thinking aptitudes. There is a range of personality-assessment instruments in the market, such as the well-known Myers-Briggs Type Indicator, based on the work of Carl Jung, and the lesser-known Enneagram, which looks at different personality types, but these instruments were not explicitly designed to provide an indication of the creative-thinking abilities of the respondent.

There are several creative-thinking assessment instruments that do provide this kind of profile although they vary greatly in their approach and in their adherence to standard testing conventions. Some have been designed to gauge whether or not a person is creative, while others were designed to recognize that everyone is creative and everyone has a unique approach to creative thinking.

Be careful of the models and assessments that classify a person as creative or noncreative. Some assessments categorize respondents into separate "creator" or "evaluator" categories. Rating some people as creative and others as noncreative and then separating people into "creative" or "noncreative" groups will not address the needs of collaborative innovation.

When discussing creative-thinking skills, there is usually a reference to the "right brain" versus "left brain" model of thinking. Roger Sperry won the 1981 Nobel Prize in Medicine for his groundbreaking work in the area of brain dominance. Each side, or hemisphere, of the brain possesses specialized and differentiated functions. The left side of the brain is thought to dominate language, logic, and scientific and analytical tasks, while the right side of the brain is thought to dominate visual, spatial, and artistic tasks. In essence, the left side deals with more details while the right side deals with more abstract processes. Over time, the right brain has become associated with creativity. Some assessment tools purport to measure the subject's tendency for "left brain" versus "right brain" thinking. You may find the value of these types of assessment tools limited. As you will soon discover, you need both sides of the brain, the "whole brain," for innovation work.

Perhaps the best assessment tool was developed by William Miller, a researcher and lecturer at Stanford University and the author of the book *Flash of Brilliance*.[1] Miller believes that everyone has the capacity to be innovative. His approach chooses not to measure whether a person is innovative, but instead seeks to understand or discover the unique way in which a person is innovative. His work encompasses the following concepts:

- We are all unique individuals. Each of us has different ways of expressing our talents, knowledge, values, and interests.
- We all have the capacity to be creative, but we express this potential differently.
- We approach innovation and change with our own unique blend of the four Innovation Styles. These four Innovation Styles are *Visioning, Exploring, Experimenting*, and *Modifying*. The styles tap into unique preferences for such things as setting clear goals, developing new rules, relying on current standards, looking to the future, working with details, and so on.

Combine Different Talents for Maximum Results

If we can discern the ways in which an individual is innovative, we will be able to leverage this capacity most effectively and efficiently for both individual and collective gain. Miller's approach supports the philosophy that everyone is creative but that everyone approaches creativity in different ways. By recognizing each person's unique talents as well as their unique Innovation Styles, we can greatly enhance both the quality of interaction within the group and the output of the group.

Many organizations have found that collaborative innovation works best when a combination of diverse thinking styles exists. An example of applying this philosophy to teamwork can be found at Nissan Design

International. In an attempt to get a wider variety of problem-solving approaches, Jerry Hirschberg hires designers in pairs—a free-form thinker alongside someone with a more analytical approach—to ensure greater intellectual diversity.[2] Other examples of leveraging diverse thinking styles can be found in the world of basketball, where Phil Jackson, the former coach of the Chicago Bulls, was able to combine the unique approaches of Michael Jordan, Dennis Rodman, and Scotty Pippin into a championship team. He repeated this winning approach with the Los Angeles Lakers, combining the diverse thinking styles of Shaq O'Neil and Kobe Bryant, among others.

Another leading contributor to the creative-thinking field is Professor Howard Gardner, who contributed his insightful theory of "Multiple Intelligences."[3] Gardner recognized that there are different types of human intelligences, including those that go beyond the traditional linguistic and mathematical intelligences that are most commonly recognized and rewarded. Gardner also offers the following different types of intelligences:

- Musical Intelligence (sound, rhythm, composition)
- Spatial Intelligence (visual aesthetics, drawing, painting)
- Kinesthetic Intelligence (dance, movement, building, drama)
- Intrapersonal Intelligence (research, reflection, personal projects)
- Interpersonal Intelligence (interactive expression, cooperative)

Your creative spirit does not have to be applied only to the linguistic and mathematical areas. Look beyond these traditional types of intelligences to see how you can bring out your unique creative talents in the other important, yet often overlooked, "multiple intelligences." Despite traditional views, many people now realize that creative thinking in the musical, spatial, kinesthetic, intrapersonal, and interpersonal areas is just as valuable as creative thinking in the traditional linguistic and mathematical areas.

Eliminate Obstacles to Creative Thinking

It is basic human nature to be curious, to try new things, and to learn by discovering new connections. But somehow, along the way, this natural creative talent has been blocked. Through self-judgment and the conditioning of others, people stop looking for new ideas, stop trying new approaches, and stop discovering new connections. Over time, their creative "muscles" weaken and in some cases, may even atrophy to the point that, when called upon, the creative muscles are so weak they are not able to jump into action.

Most barriers to creative thinking are self-imposed. You can't expect to "think outside the box" if you constantly put yourself back in the box! There are three common obstacles to creative thinking:

Obstacle 1: Hesitancy to Try New Things!

"We tried that a few years ago and it didn't work."

"We've never tried that so it won't work."

"We've always done it this way."

"We don't want any mistakes so do it the way it's always been done."

Why is it that people try many new experiences in their younger years but somehow, once they are a bit older, the number of new adventures they are willing to experience starts to dwindle? Why do they stop trying new things and want every step of the journey mapped out for them, even before they start? Perhaps people get a little too comfortable in their everyday routines. Perhaps they convince themselves that there is already too much change in the world, so in order to cope, it's best to do what they've always done.

The fear of making a mistake and the fear of what others may think can lock a person in their own creative thinking prison. Children try new things, but many adults only try new things if they think they can do them right. "I can't ski because I tried skiing once and I fell." "My job doesn't allow me to be creative." "I can't give a speech because I gave one in high school and my class didn't like it." Are these constraints real or imagined? Are these constraints still valid after all these years?

Everyone is naturally full of creativity but as Stanford Professor Michael Ray says, our "voice of judgment" takes over.[4] "You can't do that. That will never work. You'll fail. It won't be good enough.

That's the dumbest idea I've ever heard." Everyone has become very good at judging others as well as themselves. The voice of judgment creates fear and destroys confidence in people's creative talents and in their abilities to excel. They stop dreaming of what could be and see only what is reality today. These insecurities hold them back from asking new questions and taking action. What is really stopping people from being creative is not a lack of new ideas but their voice of judgment.

Creative thinkers try new things and move with the changing world. Albert Einstein determined that energy is a function of mass and velocity ($E=MC^2$), so in order to develop new creative energy, mass must be moved in some new direction! People need to move out of their comfort zones, open themselves up to new experiences and let more creativity flow into their lives. Try one thing new each week. Start with baby steps:

- Listen to a new radio station.
- Rearrange your office furniture.
- Try exotic food.
- Speak to new people. Even strangers can help people improve their creative abilities.

Also challenge yourself to really understand why you stop yourself from trying new things. Write down ten things you've always wanted to do but haven't done. What is stopping you from doing these ten things? Are your obstacles real or imagined? Alternatively, when faced with challenges from others, ask yourself if the constraints others are trying to place on you are real or imagined. How can you overcome these constraints so that you can move forward and experience new things?

Obstacle 2: "The Right Way"

"That's not the way it's done in our industry."

"Don't rock the boat."

"The board won't go for that idea. It's too radical."

So much time is spent trying to second-guess senior management and attempting to recommend the "right" answer that there is no time left to find new and better ways. As Roger Von Oech says in his book *A Whack on the Side of the Head*, many people have a tendency to stop looking for alternative right answers after the first answer has been found.[5] Stopping at the first "right" answer prevents further exploration of possible solutions. If this pattern of stopping at the first answer is repeated, the repertoire of answers soon dwindles and the ability to forge new pathways or thinking patterns in the brain is damaged. One right answer results in little room to move and too few degrees of creative freedom. As Roger Von Oech quotes Emilé Chartier, "Nothing is more dangerous than an idea when it is the only one you have."[6]

It's tough to be creative when surrounded by "one-answer" people. It's hard to work with people who are hanging on so tightly to their "right way." There are many people who presumably have the "right answer" and try to manipulate the situation so that their answer appears to be the only option. There are many people who just have to have an answer for everything, whether they're an expert in the subject area or not. Perhaps these people are so uncomfortable with not knowing that they just can't say those three little words, " I don't know." Perhaps it's hard for these people to enter the state of the unknown and leave the more comfortable state of "yes" and "no" or "right" and "wrong."

It is true that, in some situations, routine answers or the right answer may be the best. For example, at a red light, the decision to stop is commonly considered the right answer. But in other situations, ideas that are different from everyone else's, or that are different from the answers that were used in the past, are needed. The marketplace may have changed. There may be new competitors. The problems may have escalated. The budgets may be smaller. In these cases, creative answers are needed.

Strong innovation leadership is about encouraging people to look for new ways, to work outside the parameters of what's been done before to seek out new possibilities. Instead of criticizing ideas, people need to ask themselves if the idea is wrong or if the idea is just different from what they are used to. If the Wright Brothers hadn't been encouraged to go beyond the conventional wisdom that declared "humans can't fly," we might not be flying in jet aircraft today. If the Kellogg's team had not challenged the conventional wisdom that declared "cereal should be served hot," we might not be enjoying cold cereal today.

Circumstances change. Conventional wisdom evolves. The right way might not be the best approach for solving today's challenges. The right way might be based on old standards, old information, old biases, and even old wives' tales. New approaches are needed. People need to be encouraged to fly out of formation every once in a while.

If creativity is about discovering new connections, you need to evolve from allowing only "one right connection" to supporting "multiple connections." To do so:

- Increase your awareness of how you might be criticizing ideas that do not mirror your own.
- Increase your awareness of the number of different approaches you will tolerate.
- Help others increase their awareness of how they might be limiting the number of new ideas by their heavy criticism.
- Have your team adopt a phrase such as "There is more than one right way!" to be used whenever someone starts to hear too much criticism of new ideas and approaches.

Obstacle 3: We Want Control

"We never had to do that before."

"We've just finished writing the vision and mission statements. We don't want to have to change them."

"We know the old way will work."

Many people feel their lives are too chaotic and "out of control." They want the world to slow down and stop changing so much. They crave predictable routines and want answers that fit the proven patterns of the world. In reality, though, the world has never been and will never be a stable place. All things in the world, all things in life, are constantly moving and changing. The world is naturally chaotic because it is alive–it is a complex, living system that is constantly reshaping itself.

So is the corporate world. Gone are the days when "what you see today will be what you see tomorrow." Gone are the days when organizations can guarantee they will exist in fifty years and that everyone who is employed today will have a job forever. Gone are the days when the competitive set can be predicted or the distribution channel can be controlled. The political landscape is also constantly reshaping itself.

Organizations attempt to achieve stability in the midst of this chaotic change. However, once an organization stabilizes or achieves the perception of stability, most people do everything in their power to keep it that way. They spend their time and effort pursuing efficiency by perfecting current processes and approaches. Unfortunately, by the time they have perfected the process, the world has already changed and the revamped processes are already out of date.

A better strategy might be to dedicate the team's energy and skill toward finding new and more effective processes as well as building the creative-thinking skills that will be needed for coping with future challenges. While some organizations are spending their time pursuing a strategy of doing things better, others are spending their time pursuing the strategy of doing things differently. Nokia, a world leader in mobile phone technology, leapfrogged the competition by finding new and different ways to launch innovative products and services faster than the competition. In the meantime, other companies were busy reducing the number of errors in their old processes.

Creative thinking rarely emerges from organizations where order and control are valued. Organizations that are trying to control too much of their internal environment will miss out on the creative energy of their employees. If a manager tries to control all aspects of the process as well as the end result, the team will just stop searching for and finding new answers. If the ideas that receive the most support are the ones that reinforce the past and "the way we've always done things around here," the flow of new creative ideas will certainly slow down to just a trickle. It only makes sense that, if creative ideas are constantly being shot down, people will stop launching them. The overwhelming need for control leads to less exploration, less experimentation, and, in general, less creative thinking.

Noncreative thinkers are typically unwilling to let go of their opinions. They attempt to control others' viewpoints and behaviors, either overtly or passively. They do not invite others to participate in their innovative-thinking exercises. "You're new here so you probably shouldn't be involved." "You're not in our department so we don't need your input." They effectively shut off the oxygen flow to their creative vessels!

On one end of the continuum is *control* and on the other end of the continuum is *freedom.*

Control ——————— Freedom

Determine where the majority of your behavior falls: closer to the control end, where you may be stifling your own creative spirit as well as the creative spirit of those around you, or closer to the freedom end, where you may be nurturing the creative spirit and encouraging the creative juices to flow. Being aware of your behavior is a critical first step. Try to eliminate some of your controlling behavior by allowing yourself to offer new ideas as well as encouraging others to bring forward their new ideas. Realize that you could become a role model for letting go and accepting new ideas proposed by others. By doing so, you can encourage others to be a little more lenient when reviewing your new ideas in return! Learning to free your own creative spirit is an important step in building your capacity in creative thinking.

(See Chapters 3 and 7 for more ways to promote creative thinking.)

Learn to Unlearn and Forget

One of the reasons people shut down creativity is because they know that, once they have identified new ideas or new ways of doing things, they might actually have to accept and implement them. This means that they might have to change their current position. They might actually have to try new things. They might actually have to let go of "the right way" and release their grip on order and control.

As Peter Drucker once said, "If you want to do something new, you have to stop doing something old."[7] Old thinking may be covering up true creative potential. Old thinking has to be removed in order to make room for new thinking. Just as the gardener clears out old plants and weeds to make room for the sunlight to shine on the new plants, you must clear out old thinking in order to make room for new thinking. The ability to *unlearn* and the ability to *forget* some of what has been taught are fundamental skills for creative thinking. Some of the "rules" and "ways of doing things" will have to unlearned in order to make way for new ideas. (See Chapter 2 for suggestions on how to become more aware of your "rules" and assumptions.)

Accepting Failure

Remember that creative thinking also involves failure. A person should not stop trying just because perfect results are not produced on the first attempt. The game of baseball is a good of example of this. Ty Cobb's batting average was .367, which means he hit a fair ball almost four out of every ten times he was at bat. It also means he did *not* hit a fair ball six out of every ten times he was at bat. Babe Ruth's batting average was .342.

Tom Kelley of the design firm IDEO says his company's approach to experimentation is summed up in its advice to "fail often to succeed sooner."[8] Anyone in the oil exploration field can tell you that their chances of finding oil at the very first drill site are extremely low. Learning to be comfortable with a little failure in life is difficult given the social conditioning that encourages everyone to showcase achievement but certainly not the failure that might have occurred on the way to this success.

Interestingly, there was a civil engineering lab course at Penn State University that recognized and confronted the risks associated with creative behavior. The course, subtitled "Failure 101," required students to take risks and experiment in order to get a better grade; in fact, the more they "failed," the greater their chance of receiving an "A" grade in the course.

CHAPTER 2

Be Curious

The primary basis for creativity is a curious mind. GSD&M, a U.S.-based advertising agency, believes so strongly in the value of curiosity that it has engraved the word in the floor of its lobby. The agency believes that curiosity (i.e., there must be a better way) is paramount for developing creative insights and ideas.

Without curiosity, a person has great difficulty discovering new ideas. Being curious involves (a) having an open mind, (b) gaining a broader perspective, and (c) asking probing questions.

Do You Have an Open Mind?

There are many examples of people throughout history who found it difficult to have an open mind and break their existing thinking patterns. Christopher Columbus was surrounded by many such people: they believed that the earth was flat and that if he were to sail off into the distance, his convoy of ships would fall off the edge of the earth. Not too many years ago, people doubted the need for telephones. Now we have voice mail, call-waiting, call-forwarding, call-blocking, e-mail, conference calling, and mobile commerce (m-commerce). Ted Turner faced many skeptics when he introduced a twenty-four-hour news channel, CNN. Would people shift their viewing habits from the traditional six-o'clock news?

It is difficult to discover innovative solutions with a closed mind. When the mind holds onto or sets fast on one idea, it is no longer free to create. In effect, the creative mind starts to shut down. It tunes out and closes off the possibility of new discoveries.

Acknowledge That Alternative Ideas Can Exist

In order to see new ideas, we must first acknowledge that alternative ideas can exist. Why is it that we can acknowledge the presence of alternative products and services in the marketplace but block our own team's suggestions for such products and services? Why is it that we can acknowledge the appeal of new inventions in the marketplace but find it so easy to criticize new ideas that are presented within our own organizations? We need to open our minds to new possibilities, to the field of dreams. All innovations started out as simple ideas. The light bulb lighting the room you are in, the chair you are sitting on, and the shoes you are wearing were once only ideas. It took a creative thinker to bring these ideas to the world.

Being open-minded means being willing to change perceptions or "mental models" when new information surfaces. The research and development department at Pfizer Inc., the pharmaceutical company, was working on a heart drug when it discovered some amazing side effects among patients undergoing clinical trials. Low and behold, Viagra was born. It was not what they were expecting, but they were open-minded enough to see the potential in this unexpected discovery.

Make a List and Challenge Your Sacred Traditions

Often, progress is blocked by our sacred traditions: our opinions, assumptions, or rules of "the way it's done." While some sacred traditions may be valuable to maintain, others may be hindering the innovation process by preventing new ideas from surfacing. What if Howard Schultz (of Starbucks) had never challenged the sacred tradition that people will only pay a dollar for a cup of coffee?

Sacred traditions may no longer be relevant for today's thinking or marketplace. "New opportunities rarely fit the way an industry has always approached the market, defined it or organized to serve it."[1] Don't let the way things have been done in the past dictate, and therefore predetermine, the way things will be done in the future. Open your mind by challenging your sacred traditions.

Robert Kriegel first referred to this concept as "sacred cows," which he defines as " . . . outmoded beliefs, assumptions, practices, policies, systems, strategies that inhibit change and prevent responsiveness to new opportunities."[2] Likewise, Peter Senge refers to our "mental models" as potential barriers to finding new and possibly more appropriate ways to deal with the changing world.[3]

Industries are often disrupted by new players who see the potential in new business models where the traditional players do not. Here are some examples of ways in which creative thinkers challenged sacred traditions:

- Japanese car manufacturers made cars smaller when American car manufacturers believed they should be larger.
- Linux encouraged programmers to improve its free, open-source operating system while other software developers held on tightly to their proprietary systems.
- Southwest Airlines encourages "sit where you want" open seating, challenging the conventional idea of preassigned seating.
- Fast Company magazine challenged the traditional staid tone of business magazines by presenting business articles in a short, exciting, and visually appealing manner.

Many sacred traditions are activities that no one has ever stopped to question. Many of them may be non-value-added things that your team spends time doing—time that could be reallocated to more productive activities! Here are some of the sacred traditions I have heard over the years:

- "Everyone needs a copy of everything."
- "We only fund new ideas once a year, at budget time."
- "We're a food company so we only look at opportunities inside the food industry."
- "If it doesn't work in the United States, it probably won't work elsewhere."
- "If we can't show a financial return in two years, we won't receive the funding."
- "We define the industry the same way everyone else does."

A good innovation leader creates an environment where these sacred traditions can be challenged and addressed. In order to challenge these sacred traditions, you must first be aware of them. Begin by making a list of the industry's sacred traditions. Decide which ones are helpful and which ones are blocking innovation. Then make a list of your own organization's sacred traditions. Challenge the fundamental thinking that drives your business.

Hold Your Criticism Until You Hear the Idea's Potential

It seems that the more a person perceives himself to be an expert in a certain field, the more resistant he is to listening to alternative ideas. Whatever the idea, if it doesn't fit with his preselected solution, it is discarded without consideration. (Perhaps he perceives a loss of power if the current system is disrupted by the acceptance of the new idea.)

Progress is impossible if you keep doing what you've always done. Show you have an open mind by slowing down long enough to hear the potential of the idea before you jump all over it.

Gain a Broader Perspective

Ideas and solutions are everywhere. How broad is the idea-gathering process in your organization? Are you actively scouting out different perspectives from a variety of sources, from people outside your company, from people in other industries or government agencies, from people from other countries? Are you casting the net wide enough?

Let Outsiders Bring in Ideas

Widen the search for ideas to the far corners of the organization where great ideas may be hidden. While at Kraft General Foods, I asked over 500 people within the organization to contribute their ideas for a new cereal brand. The response was overwhelming and proved to me that people are just waiting to be asked for their ideas and to make a contribution.

Why not ask the "experts" for their perspective? If the problem has to do with suitcases, ask the airline baggage handlers. If the problem has to do with food, ask restaurant chefs. If the problem has to do with education, ask teachers, students, and parents. They have a lot of fresh insight that could help you quickly identify new ideas.

Why not look at international companies? An organization that profited immensely by gaining a different perspective on its world is Loblaws Companies Limited, a leading supermarket chain in Canada. Faced with the challenge of improving its private-label program, the Loblaws team embarked on a journey to discover the best products and marketing techniques from around the world. One of their first stops was England, where they analyzed Tesco, Sainsbury, and Marks & Spencer, who were already ahead of the game in selling upscale private-label grocery products. They also visited many restaurants around the world and begged the great chefs to share their secret recipes. Upon their return to Canada, they developed what would become one of the strongest private-label programs in the world, branded under the President's Choice label. Gaining a different perspective by asking experts for their insights certainly did wonders for the Loblaws team.[4]

Why not ask people unrelated to the problem for their perspective? Teams often suffer from "industry think," where everyone in the industry is following the same rules, looking at the market the same way, and, in general, thinking and acting along the same lines. Everyone is assuming the industry works a certain way, and they may, therefore, be blind to new opportunities. Individuals and groups alike can benefit from knowing and tapping into a rich diversity of thought. Creativity needs people of all shapes and sizes. That's why the design firm IDEO intermixes disciplines and functions on its creativity teams. According to Tom Kelley, a key ingredient of a hot group is that "the team is well rounded and respectful of diversity . . . and is drawn from widely divergent disciplines."[5]

Conversations with diverse people spark creative thinking. Expand your contact to include zookeepers, architects, martial artists, pilots, auctioneers, teachers, and neighborhood children. Ask someone who doesn't know your challenges for fresh advice. Expand your bandwidth to receive ideas from wherever, whenever, they choose to appear! You never know if that random act of searching the Web or sitting beside someone on the airplane or standing in line at the bank will result in a conversation that leads to a great idea.

Dig a Little Deeper to Understand These Perspectives

Everyone views the same situation from his or her own perspective. How one sees things is determined by one's own unique personality, past experiences, and prejudices. The jury system relies on twelve jurors instead of only one so that the issue of guilt or innocence can be viewed from different perspectives. Most sports use more than one referee so that the odds of seeing the "full picture" increase. No one person can see the entire situation. There are always blind spots. Sometimes being too close to a situation or being tied to one solution can prevent new solutions from being seen.

There are often hundreds of ways to look at a problem. Sort through the range of facts, memories, emotions, observations, perceptions, and impressions. Turn the problem around and look at it from new angles. For example, a marketing team was challenged to identify a revised brand-positioning and marketing strategy for a prominent pharmaceutical product. Using the broader-perspectives approach, they first made a list of the different customer groups for the brand and then determined what their respective needs were. The needs of the patients (reliability, comfort), their families (information), their pharmacists (information, ease of dispensing, and profit), their physicians (up-to-date information on both the drug itself and other products that might be reliable substitutes), the nurses and intensive care unit staff (information on dispensing and recommended patient care), and the payer, such as the insurance company or government agency (cost, comparative products, risk of complications from taking the particular drug) were all considered. By taking a broader-perspective approach in determining the various customer-group needs, the team was able to identify different areas that could represent exciting new strategies and new programs that, in turn, could differentiate its business from the competition. This approach also helped the team assess what percentage of the marketing budget should be allocated to communicating with each customer group.

Build Your Observation Skills

Seeing the world from different angles is like shining a flashlight beam on different areas in the room. The more one moves around, the more parts of the room one can see. Observing an aircraft-landing from a cockpit is a lot different from watching the landing from the ground. Observing a school of fish while scuba diving is a lot different from looking at the surface of the water from a boat. Seeing North America from an Asian perspective is a lot different from seeing it from an American perspective. Too often, one falls in love with one's own view of the world. Innovators can benefit from seeing the world from beyond the usual boundaries—beyond departments, organizations, industries, and countries.

There is a difference between looking at something and actually seeing what is there! The mind automatically filters information. A person can look at something and not really see it. It's like driving down a country road on a dark night with the headlights on. People can see what's in their path in front of them, but they miss a lot of interesting scenery around them. In order to see more, people need to override the mind's filter and force themselves to be more observant. Great artists like Georgia O'Keeffe mastered this technique by being able to see more details in a simple object, such as a flower, than most others could see. Sam Walton, the founder of Wal-Mart, made it a habit when visiting his competitor's stores to look at the details and find at least one idea or example to take back to his organization.

Developing a curious mind requires better observation skills. Practice trying to "see more." For example, when you are sitting in a restaurant, waiting in an airport lounge, or standing in line at the bank, observe more. How is the restaurant organized? How are the tables and chairs arranged? Where is the kitchen and where are the busing stations? Why did they organize the seating the way they did? How do the waiters serve other customers? How could the serving process be improved? At the airport, how are the check-in counters organized? How could the process of checking-in and boarding the airplane be improved? How could the process be more enjoyable and more exciting? At the bank, how could the deposit and withdrawal processes be improved? Play with your observations and ideas.

Another way to gain a different perspective is to use a video camera to record, with permission of course, customers' actions with particular products or services. By "walking a mile in their shoes," an observer can find out how the product or service is perceived by the customer and where improvements might be needed. Record the team's actions on the factory floor or selling floor to find new ideas. Pay attention to the details. The more you observe, the more you see. The more you listen, the more you hear.

Write down new insights. There is a constant flow of insights and ideas in the brain. If you don't capture these thoughts, they might be lost forever somewhere in the cerebral cortex. Keep a small pad of paper in the car, in the bathroom, in the kitchen, beside the bed—or carry a PalmPilot. You never know when and where that brilliant insight will surface!

Focused observation can help build creative thinking skills. Try these observation exercises:

- List five things you noticed on your way to work today.
- Describe the floor plan of the entrance or lobby in your building.
- With your eyes closed, name three objects close to you that are blue.

- Next time you watch a commercial on television, wait two minutes and then try to recall the commercial and remember the name of the product being advertised in the commercial.

Ask Probing Questions

"Judge a man by his questions rather than his answers."

—VOLTAIRE

You cannot be a curious thinker if you are afraid to ask questions. My mentors at Procter & Gamble taught me to ask probing questions and not to be afraid to ask again if the person avoided answering the original question. The acceptance of this type of questioning was the norm in the Procter & Gamble culture, but it is not the norm in many other organizational cultures. Some people have been taught not to ask questions, especially of their elders or of people in positions of power for fear of embarrassing them. This is a hurdle that needs to be overcome if the creative spirit is to flourish.

Enjoy Asking Questions

"Why don't we have soft drink dispensers in our homes?"

"When did human beings first wear watches?"

"How does a PalmPilot work? Who invented it?"

"Where does my garbage go after the truck picks it up at my residence?"

"Why don't psychics ever win lotteries?"

"Why is the slowest time of the day for traffic called rush-hour?"

"Why can't we file our income taxes every two years instead of every year?"

Columbo, the brilliant detective played on television by Peter Falk, would say in every episode, "Excuse me ma'am. Just one more question." The more questions he asked, the more information he had to solve the case. Become a creative-thinking detective! Ask probing questions. There is no such thing as a wasted question. You will always learn something. Take the time to question the "facts" in any situation by asking more questions. Write down what is known about the problem, what information is available, and what information is not available. Ask tougher questions.

- Who could put us out of business?
- If we were on the executive team, what would we do in this situation?
- What would really shake up this industry?
- Why aren't we doing anything about this?

The Creative-Thinking Mantra: "Why? What If? What Else?"

The three curiosity questions that push individuals the farthest into new territory are the following simple questions: "Why? What if? What else?"

"Why?" is the best of these three questions. By asking "Why," you are exploring the rationale behind a given approach and opening up the possibility that there might be an alternative approach. Ask questions such as "Why?" "Why are we doing this?" "Why are we doing this like this?" For example, "Why do we have sales contests?" "Why do we need to prepare this report if no one is reading it?" "Why do we need to spend so much on packaging materials?"

While at Kraft General Foods, I started the "Why Group." The objective of the Why Group was to encourage more questioning of our business strategies in hopes of identifying more innovative ways to build our businesses. The Why Group attracted many participants from different divisions of the company who would meet over lunch once a month to discuss a particularly tough business challenge. The owner of the challenge would provide a brief background sketch of the problem, and then the other participants would ask "Why" questions to find the different angles of the problem. Through this inquiry, we were able to identify creative new ideas to strengthen the businesses—all based on the question "Why?" Encourage a community of "Why?" inquirers in your organization. Why not start a Why Group of your own?

The YY (Double Why) Question

As Socrates demonstrated over 2000 years ago, great insights come from asking good questions. A good leader does not need to know all the answers. She needs to know the questions to ask. Creative thinking begins with great questions, not answers. Great creative thinkers stay with the question instead of rushing to find an immediate solution. They ask more questions than the average person and are comfortable in the often uncomfortable situation of not immediately having the answer. This is the test of a true creative thinker. While society has reinforced the notion that the first person to come up with a witty answer must be the smartest, in truth, many breakthroughs have come after much contemplation and investigation. For example, Thomas Edison said, "I haven't failed. I've just come up with 1,000 ways not to make a light bulb." He constantly questioned his assumptions to look for deeper insights. Barbara Walters, the famous journalist, rarely hits the jackpot on the first question. Her success stems from her aptitude for relentless questioning, repeating questions from various angles, digging deeper and deeper until magic insights reveal themselves.

Don't be satisfied with surface answers. Jumping to the solution too quickly results in mediocre ideas or ideas that don't fit the needs of the real problem. Keep asking the "Why?" questions and dig for more details. In order to unpeel the layers of packaging to get to the real heart of the matter, it is necessary to repeat the question. For example, ask "Why?" and then ask "Why?" again and again until you uncover new insights. "Why do we do it like this?" "Because we've always done it like this." "Why do we always do it like this?" "Because that's the way it's done in our industry." "Why do we want to do it like all our competition?" "Because, well, I don't know. You've got a good point!"

In another example, the problem may appear to be poor sales revenue. When asked why the revenue was so low, someone might answer that there is new competition or that the price is too high or that there aren't enough salespeople. Choose one of these answers—the price is too high—and ask *why* the price is too high. The answer may be because the prices were raised by 12 percent each year. The next step would be to investigate the strategy behind the annual increase and to challenge the 12-percent increase. Why not 3 percent or 5 percent or 10 percent? Asking "Why?" questions helps everyone look at the problem from different angles and encourages a deeper dialogue as to what the real issue may be. If this investigation stage was missed, the team might have jumped to the conclusion that the problem was caused by lack of salespeople and gone off looking for more resources to hire more people, instead of investigating the other angles of the issue.

In addition to the "Why? What If? What Else?" mantra and the YY question, you may find the list of probing questions in Appendix B helpful.

Of course, there are always two parts of asking any question: the asking and the listening. Make sure that you also hear the answers!

CHAPTER 3

Discover New Connections

Try this simple exercise created by a colleague, Mari Messer. Take a piece of paper. For the next two minutes, write down the names of all the people you know. Try it! Start listing them. Now stop. Look at the your list of names. Explain how your list flowed from the first name to the last name. See the jumps and connections your mind made as you thought of more and more names.

Here is my list: *Alex, Dad, Mary, John, Maureen (members of the family), Jilly, Anna, Bonnie (children in the family), Laura (Bonnie's friend in London), Lori, Bill (my friends in London), Jake (their son), Jake (the principal at my grade school), Mrs. Birch (my kindergarten teacher), etc.* How did my mind get from Alex to Mrs. Birch? My mind hopped and jumped and made new connections!

This exercise illustrates the technique used in many creative-thinking exercises: *Pursue a large quantity of ideas and make connections between these ideas.* The great connection could arrive at the second or eighth or thirtieth idea. One never knows when a great idea will arrive.

You need to force yourself past your first or second association to find more ideas. A football coach rarely asks his team to run the same play time after time. Instead, the coach finds new ways to connect the players on the field to outwit the opposing team. By combining and recombining different player movements, the coach is able to devise creative ways to out-maneuver their opponents. Just as the photographer who takes many pictures before she finds the best one, or the cartoonist who draws many cartoons until he sees the one he likes, creative thinkers need to identify many ideas and uncover as many connections as they can.

Creative thinkers tap into their imaginations by combining and recombining different ideas or concepts to make new connections. Creative thinking is really about discovering new connections through the use of (1) the imagination, (2) diverse stimuli, and (3) Creative-Connections Powertools.

Using Your Imagination

Albert Einstein once said, "Imagination is more important than knowledge." The Concise Oxford dictionary defines imagination as the "mental faculty of forming images or concepts of external objects not present to the senses," and "the creative faculty of the mind." Without imagination, there wouldn't be airplanes, spaghetti, e-mail, *The Lion King*, or microwave ovens!

In today's world, it is no longer enough to do the same thing as the competition. As the boundaries between countries, industries, and market segments crumble, everyone is facing a plethora of competition. In order to stand out from the crowd, you must be able to see something distinctly new and better than what others are seeing and then, of course, you must put this new insight into action.

Mental ruts can form over time. The same thought patterns get "wired" into the mind through repetition. When new information is introduced, it is either slotted into the existing pattern or massaged and twisted until it fits. Often, the new information is rejected outright because it doesn't seem to fit. Creative thinkers override these set patterns by burning new pathways in their brains.

Here are several ways to burn new pathways and strengthen your imagination:

■ **Imagine more than one use for your product or service.**

Children are great at transforming objects into new ideas. Watch them transform a soft drink can into a microphone or pasta into a necklace. They play with ideas to see the possibilities that lie within. A common warm-up exercise for strengthening creative-thinking skills is "name five uses for a rubber band or a paperclip." Why not try a more imaginative exercise such as naming ten alternative uses for your soup product or your delivery service or your manufacturing waste? We can all take a page from the Starbucks manual and admire the number of alternative coffee drinks they can make from a shot of espresso!

■ **Use your imagination to push the boundaries of what is commonplace.**

Imagination is a higher form of thinking. Imagine turning a commonplace object like a rock into a "pet" and marketing it as "maintenance-free and easy to train." Gary Dahl actually invented the pet rock in 1975 and sold over five million before the craze dissolved.[1] Now that's imagination!

■ **Use your imagination to do the opposite of what is expected.**

Until 1968, most high jumpers used the scissor-kick or front-roll techniques for clearing the high-jump bar. Then along came Dick Fosbury, who cleared the bar the opposite way, using the back flop. His radical backward style, nicknamed the Fosbury Flop, won him the gold medal at the Olympics and redefined the sport of high jumping forever.

■ **Look to other industries or areas for inspiration.**

Fosbury's idea of flipping backward in the air was not new—it was just new to high jumping. Divers throw their bodies backward through the air, so why can't high jumpers? Connecting an idea from one sport to another sport can result in a breakthrough. Look beyond your particular company or industry to find new ideas.

■ **Imagine the wildest idea you can and then tame this wild idea.**

If, for example, your challenge were to redesign a car so that people could eat fast food in it more comfortably, you might want to begin by stretching your imagination to find your wildest idea. Your wildest idea might be to put a picnic table in the car. From here, you could tame this idea and identify several more useful ideas such as a fold-down mini-table or a small table or food caddy between the two front seats.

Some people have a hard time suspending judgment and playing with new ideas. "What's the purpose in playing? We don't have time to play" are the comments most often heard from uptight people. Learning how to "play" with ideas relaxes the mind long enough to allow new pathways to be built. Play is a critical component of strengthening the imagination for creative thinking.

Encourage all team members to use their imaginations. "Every other year in the fall, Honda of Japan holds a contest where employees use company money to develop ideas for new vehicles and transportation concepts. Practicality is not necessarily a criterion for success. Prizes awarded include the Mechanical Prize, the Dream Prize, the Nice Idea Prize, and the Unique Prize. The spectators also award the Golden Icon Prize for the most popular idea."[2]

One last note on imagination: Imagination is not constrained by a lack of resources. People often use the lack of resources as an excuse for not having new ideas or taking action. The movie *The Blair Witch Project* is a good example of imagination on a low budget. In an industry characterized by big budgets and Hollywood stars, Haxan Films invested only a few thousand dollars, and Artisan Entertainment, which bought the film and distributed it throughout the world, only invested $1 million. This low-budget film went on to gross over $100 million in sales. In addition to being a low-budget film, it was also the first film to be marketed heavily through the Internet rather than through the mainstream media. This example shows that imagination can go a long way in overcoming a lack of resources.

Use Diverse Stimuli

Stimuli are a key ingredient for making new connections. Many people try to come up with new ideas from a blank slate. They stare at a blank piece of paper or flipchart and hope that Eureka! a bolt of lightning will strike them, and a breakthrough idea will magically appear on the page. While that might work for some people some of the time, most people need to jumpstart the process with the raw ingredient of creativity—other ideas. If 98 percent of ideas already exist in one form or another, the answers must already exist somewhere. All one needs to do is find them and then combine and recombine them in a unique way that makes them work in solving a new challenge. In the "cycle of ideas," all or at least most ideas are reincarnated from a previous life in some other company, agency, industry, or country.

- **Decide what type of stimuli you need—related or unrelated.**

Bring back fresh insights that can be used as stimuli for growing new ideas. The type of stimuli needed depends on the particular problem and the team's unique approach to solving problems. For some problems or situations, the team might want to seek out related stimuli. For example, if the team is looking for ideas to improve the school's fundraising efforts, they might want to look at other schools' fundraising efforts as well as at examples from other nonprofit organizations (such as the Canadian Heart and Stroke Foundation or the Red Cross). The team might want to bring in examples of previous programs and advertisements from other fundraising campaigns as stimuli for fresh connections.

Alternatively, the team might want to seek out unrelated stimuli. For example, they might want to look at how banks attract new customers, how lotteries are conducted, or how the Army recruits new soldiers, in order to find new insights that could help them design a better fundraising program. The team can list the attributes of these programs and then use their imagination to connect these attributes with the specific challenges of their own fundraising program.

For some people, using related stimuli is preferable because it represents a direct approach to creative thinking and is perhaps more concrete. Such people are able to see the links between the stimuli and their particular challenge more easily and therefore can make easier connections to what they feel will be useful ideas. But for some, using related stimuli is too limiting. They want to stretch themselves into new territory and enjoy the creative-thinking exercise of linking unrelated stimuli to the challenge at hand. These people may have an easier time with abstract thinking and are therefore better able to see new connections easily. Others may not be able to make these connections with unrelated stimuli as easily and end up frustrated. If you are working alone, chose the type of stimuli that works best for you. If you are working in a team, vary the mixture of creative-thinking exercises using related and unrelated stimuli so that you tap into everyone's unique preferences. Either way, experience has shown that all teams benefit from using some type of stimuli, whether related or unrelated, rather than using none.

■ **Look internally as well as externally for diverse stimuli.**

The largest source of fresh ideas is employees and other internal stakeholders. Pay attention to front-line staff and new employees, whose fresh insights are extremely valuable. Listen to employees in other departments. Many people have a lot of information to share but don't share it because "no one asked." Try talking to other departments or business units or holding cross-functional innovation groups to see if they can offer a fresh perspective. Also review previous programs to find old ideas that can be reused in a new way. Ideas that might not have worked in the past due to underfunding, competitive conditions, or poor implementation might work now. Why not hold industry seminars once a month to update everyone on what's happening in the industry, what's working, and what's not working?

Creative thinkers also capture ideas from a variety of external sources. They know others may have faced similar challenges in some other company, in some other industry, in some other government agency, or in some other country. They know the ingredients for their solutions are out there somewhere.

So get out of the office! Visit interesting places. The marketing team at Kraft General Foods looked for new cereal-marketing ideas at the New York Toy Show, which also happened to be a fun place to visit. Visit the Alden B. Dow "Hall of Ideas" in Midland, Michigan, a wonderful museum that combines fact, fiction, art, and science to offer a very stimulating array of ideas. Try searching for insights at cross-industry conferences and tradeshows. The Internet also represents a deep and rich pool of ideas. Figure 3-1 is a list of alternative sources of diverse stimuli.

Figure 3-1. Sources of diverse stimuli.

Historical review	Television	The mall
Children	Old files	Paint colors
List of trends	Travel	Other companies
Photos	Complaints	Ads
Opinions	Catalogs	Children's books
Intuition	Factory	Competition
Nursing homes	Construction site	Retail
Greeting cards	Atlas	International
News articles	On the bus	At the beach
Airport	Thesaurus	Flyers
Your desk	Trade shows	Toy store
Junk mail	Video store	At the zoo
Magazines	Other departments	On campus
Grocery store	Videos	New people
Cookbook	Dictionary	Bar drink guide
Internet	Flea market	Library

■ **Start today to develop a more systemized approach to collecting and sharing diverse stimuli.**

The simplest way to collect new ideas generated from stimuli is, obviously, to write them down. Carry a small idea notebook or use a PalmPilot to capture these fleeting thoughts, or they might disappear forever. Lots of great ideas surface during meetings. Where do they go? Make sure the team develops an idea-capture system such an Innovation Bank or Idea Bank so that these ideas can be referenced at a later date. Make it easy for people to access the rich data hidden in company files, including all those ideas generated in previous brainstorming sessions or findings from market research reports. Don't let ideas get lost simply because of employee turnover.

A significant challenge facing many organizations is the loss of institutional memory with turnovers, retirement, and yes, downsizing. Employees are leaving with rich data. In the North American public-service sector, close to one in five employees will be retiring over the next few years. That is an incredible knowledge and experience base that will soon be walking out the door. While organizations are often focused on creating new knowledge, they might be overlooking old knowledge that needs to be collected and shared.

Many companies excel at using their Intranet or informal channels to let others know who's who so that everyone knows how best to access information. It's still amazing, however, how fragmented many organizations continue to be—there are places where people don't know their fellow employees. All members of an organization have experience, knowledge, and unique perspectives that need to be brought together and leveraged for collective benefit. The largest source of new ideas might be the employees, so the communication channels between departments should be opened. Cross-train employees in other departments so that they understand the organization from many angles and can help coworkers with additional insights.

Consider accessing electronic tools, such as e-mail, groupware idea-generation and decision-making programs, the organization's Intranet, the Internet and Extranet (a network designed to connect your broader enterprise, including suppliers and customers) as well as setting up a call center to process new ideas. Hallmark Cards is an example of a company that is using advanced groupware tools such as Communispace to foster collaboration with employees and customers.

To avoid "reinventing the wheel," identify common or repetitive aspects of your team's projects and develop a process and idea bank to help jumpstart these projects. For example, if your team is constantly looking for new ideas to promote your product or service, you might want to start collecting examples of promotions—contests, coupons, sampling methods, special events, etc.—to be used to jumpstart creative thinking for the new project. Emmperative.com uses this philosophy for idea generation as the foundation for developing systemized marketing processes and idea banks for several leading organizations including Procter & Gamble and the Coca-Cola Company.

A team might want to consider implementing a more formal approach to sharing and showcasing new ideas within the organization. Nortel Networks recently established a Share and Discover Day where, for twenty-four hours, it used its Web technology to share its latest programs and highlight guest speakers. Hewlett-Packard Printer Division recently put together a traveling trailer museum that highlighted the evolution of the inkjet technology. The museum was shipped to many places so that people could benefit from learning the history of, as well as the potential for, inkjet technology. Sodexho Marriott also conducted a traveling innovation forum in which it showcased innovation that was relevant to furthering its business strategy in addition to providing training in Innovation Management. The best ideas for customer retention, customer service, and human-resource development are highlighted at this forum.

Using the Ten Creative-Connections Powertools

The mind is full of ideas from past experiences and from observations gained through television or conversations. Some people rely on their subconscious mind to access these ideas. But, unfortunately, they never know when these ideas might surface–it could be early in the morning, late at night, on a walk, or in the shower. Other people prefer to take a more structured approach to finding new ideas, using specific tools and techniques. In David Letterman fashion, here are the Top Ten Creative-Connections Powertools.

Creative-Connections Powertool 10: Rummaging in the Attic

Description of This Creative-Connections Powertool. There are many great ideas simply sitting in the "attics of our minds" as well as in the "attics of our organizations." We have a tendency to trash the past and hold the perception that an idea from five years ago will be of little use in helping to solve our current challenge. However, elements of previous solutions or ideas can prove to be very valuable fuel for jumpstarting our idea engines. Look at ideas such as bell-bottom jeans, disco music, scooters, pogo sticks, and roller skates, all of which have resurfaced.

How to Implement This Creative-Connections Powertool. The first step is to discover what is in the attic. Find those old ideas and dust them off. Interview others who have previously worked on the same challenges, and learn from their experiences. Excavate old research reports, previous brainstorming-session reports, and old business plans. Unearth the rich reservoir of idea starters. Ask the knowledge-management folks to establish a link to the database of information relating to the challenge. Access the team's idea bank on the Intranet, if they have one. Uncover what is already there and reconnect it in a new way to your current problem or challenge. Attic ideas are also great idea starters for any meeting. Ask the participants to submit their top attic ideas before the meeting and then begin the meeting by distributing a list of these ideas.

Creative-Connections Powertool 9: Cultivating Obsession

Description of This Creative-Connections Powertool. The best way to find new ideas for a certain product, service, or process is to become obsessed with the challenge. IDEO, the California-based design company, believes in this approach. At the beginning of all projects, the members of the design team take the time to understand the market, the client, the technology, and the perceived constraints of the problem. They observe real people in real-life situations to find out what makes them tick—what confuses them, what they like, what they hate, and where they have latent needs not addressed by current products and services. For example, if they were faced with the challenge of inventing a better shopping cart, they would immerse themselves in the state of grocery shopping, shopping carts, and any and all possible relevant technologies. They observe and understand how people shop and the challenges they face with shopping and shopping carts.[3]

How to Implement This Creative-Connections Powertool. Being obsessed with the challenge requires one to "live and breathe the challenge." It means interviewing the "experts" and observing actual customer behavior. It means learning about the origins of the challenge and investigating it from all angles. Seek out all the information—all the facts, opinions, samples, and reviews you can find on the subject. For example, if you were faced with designing a new beer brand, you could obsess with the following:

- Understanding the current state of the market to discover which brands sell the most, in which regions, in which months, to which customer groups.

- Understanding the bigger picture of the global beer market by conducting an Internet search of all the beer Web sites in order to understand the appeal of unique segments and unique brands in other countries.

- Interviewing brewmasters to understand the history of beer, beer recipes, and the source of beer ingredients.

- Interviewing other "beer experts," such as sales managers, bartenders, and customers to understand their needs and their desires for current and new beer brands.

- Reviewing consumer research studies and observing customers in bars and restaurants.

- Investigating other beverage categories to understand the trends in these categories.

- And, of course, personally sampling a wide variety of beer so that you have first-hand knowledge of the category!

In another example, if a team were faced with the challenge of buying new equipment for a production line, they shouldn't limit themselves to reviewing one or two sales brochures. They should ask others for their opinions and search the Internet for other opinions. They might find that one of the suppliers is working on a new model that could lead the team to postpone its decision for a while until the new technology is introduced. Obsession will definitely lead to better insights.

Creative-Connections Powertool 8: Analyzing Frustrations

Description of This Creative-Connections Powertool. "Solving customer problems sparks innovation."[4] One of the most fertile areas for identifying new ideas is discovering what frustrates others about the current product, service, or process. While it is always great to focus on what is wonderful, the team might want to take a quick look at what is not so wonderful. In the field of innovative thinking, it is sometimes these very deficiencies that are the origin of a breakthrough idea.

A great example of a company that benefited from understanding its customers' frustrations is Black & Decker. People were frustrated at needing to have a partner hold the flashlight or needing a prop on which to place the flashlight while they worked on a specific task. The frustration grew if the person or the flashlight moved so that the light no longer shone on the area where the customer was working. Black & Decker focused on this customer frustration and invented the Snakelight, a flashlight that could be twisted around a ladder or another object to stay in position until the task was done.

FedEx solved many of the frustrations customers had with courier services. Not only did it address the frustration of late packages with its "absolutely positively has to get there overnight" service, it also addressed the frustration a customer felt when they didn't know the location of their package. FedEx responded with its revolutionary online tracking system. Now all customers can track their package's journey so that both the sender and the recipient know the package's location at any time and its expected time of arrival.

Here's a frustration that is yet to be solved: In any large city, there is an increasing incidence of road rage and red-light runners. A high percentage of accidents occur at intersections during the time when the traffic lights are changing. Why haven't car manufacturers discovered that their consumers need brake lights at the front as well as the back of their car? Front brake lights would help lower the number of accidents at intersections because a driver would no longer have to guess whether the oncoming car would stop or proceed into the intersection. This kind of frustration or complaint can be a rich source for creating breakthrough ideas for redesigning cars.

How to Implement This Creative-Connections Powertool. Have the courage to ask customers to share their frustrations. Ask them what frustrates them about your products, services, or processes as well as those of the competitors. Discover what features are missing. Discover what other products or services they need to combine with yours in order to get the job done. In essence, find out everything about their frustrations.

Creative-Connections Powertool 7: Identifying the Gold Standard

Description of This Creative-Connections Powertool. Whatever your challenge, you know there are other people who have faced a similar challenge. The concept of the Gold Standard Powertool is to seek out those people and organizations that have solved a similar challenge in an outstanding way. In doing so, they are revered as the Gold Standard in this particular area, be it product development, advertising, customer service, or cross-industry collaboration.

How to Implement This Creative-Connections Powertool. Identify organizations that have achieved excellence in your particular challenge area. For example, if you are looking for new ideas for "organizing customer flow," you might want to investigate what Disney has done to organize their customer flow so everything runs smoothly at their theme parks or what McDonald's has done in order to serve their customers quickly. If you are looking for ideas for advertising, you might want to look at examples of recent award-winning advertisements. If you are looking for ideas for recruiting new employees, you might want to see how many of the top organizations recruit students or how NBA teams recruit star basketball players. A literature search and Internet key word search are very valuable resources, as are direct interviews.

Once you have identified the gold-standard organization, make a list of the elements of the process or program that made this organization into your gold standard. Relate these elements back to your particular situation and discuss which elements would be useful. Determine what action steps would be needed to implement these elements in your organization.

Creative-Connections Powertool 6: Adopting and Adapting

Description of This Creative-Connections Powertool. Great ideas already exist somewhere else in the universe. All you need to do is find them and adopt them as your own. Find out what others are doing well. Don't limit the stimuli to your own company and only "fast adapt" ideas from within the four walls of your own organization.

How to Implement This Creative-Connections Powertool. There are several sources for adopted ideas. First, *look within your own organization*—in other departments, regions, or business units. Many companies spend so much time reinventing the wheel in separate parts of the organization when all they need to do is ask another department how they solved a similar challenge. What better place to find ideas to adopt than from your own relatives?

Second, *study competitors' products or services* or, in the case of a government agency, other agency services and programs. Keep an eye out for emerging competitors, those small but growing entities that are on the move. Companies like Coca-Cola and Pepsi can benefit from keeping their eyes on the new beverage players as valuable sources of new ideas. Organizations like the United States Forest Service can benefit from keeping their eyes on environmental lobbying groups and logging companies to better understand the upcoming challenges as well as potential new solutions.

Investigate your competitors' products in other countries that might soon be imported to your country. Check the trademark applications being submitted by the competitors. One of the first indications of their plans to bring a new product or service into the market is a trademark application.

While adopting ideas from within the category might be beneficial, adopting ideas from *outside the category* and bringing these ideas to the category before others do, would definitely put you ahead of the game. It's best to venture outside the category, or as Jon Pearson, a creativity consultant, likes to say, "do a little off-road thinking." Look to neighboring categories to adopt new ideas. For example, for a challenge in the beer market, look at the neighboring categories of substitute products such as wine, liquor, and soft drinks. Find out what new ideas are working in these categories. Find out what it would take to switch consumers of these substitute products to your product or product category. Or better yet, develop a new category that bridges both your category and this neighboring category, such as wine/soft-drink combinations or beer/soft-drink combinations.

Other ideas can be found in organizations that have faced similar challenges. These organizations do not have to be in the same category, in the same country, or even in the neighboring categories. A cafeteria manager for Sodexho Marriott developed an Easy Pass system where customers could easily deposit $5 in the jar to pay for their meals and bypass the cashier line. He got the idea while driving on the highway and realizing that cars with the E-Z Pass or the correct change could sail through the tollbooth, while others had to wait to get change from the cashier. Here are some other examples of possible creative cross-industry learning ideas:

- Banks could adopt the numbering system many bakeries and government offices use to serve customers so that their banking customers could sit and relax while waiting their turn.

- Theater designers could adopt the Nike shoe air-pump technology in their seat design so customers could pump up their seats to make themselves more comfortable during a performance.

- Restaurants could adopt the technique used by Walt Disney World to fully integrate a theme into all elements of a chosen design, including menu items, décor, cutlery, pricing, staff uniforms, and advertising.

Most companies look head-to-head only with competitors in their own category. Innovators, however, look beyond the borders of their category to find new ideas to adopt and adapt.

Creative-Connections Powertool 5: Combining Ideas

Description of This Creative-Connections Powertool. Creative thinking is a bit like cooking: a little of this and a little of that. Creative thinkers are aware of the objects or ideas around them and look for new connections through combining diverse objects or ideas. Children playing house use whatever blankets, boxes, toys, cushions, newspapers, or other objects are around and combine them into a great playhouse. Creative executives at advertising agencies are good at this as well. They look for combinations and links using such things as current movies or fashion trends as the basis for new ad proposals. Artists use mixed media to create new works of wonder. Software programmers mix and match different technologies to find new ways to program our lives. McDonald's was one of the first fast-food restaurants to introduce value combos: a combination of sandwich, fries, and drink.

How to Implement This Creative-Connections Powertool. Practice combining objects in everyday life. How could a computer keyboard be combined with a printer? How could a doctor's office be combined with a school? How could the concept of a "book-of-the-month club" be combined with wine? What else could be combined with your product, service, or program? Seemingly unrelated stimuli can be forced back into a combination with the product or service. Open your mind to the possibilities. Experiment.

Creative-Connections Powertool 4: Finding Similarities

Description of This Creative-Connections Powertool. When you are faced with a creative challenge, a good technique is to think of other challenges that might be similar. For example, find similarities in nature: How is the organization like a tree, or how is the process like a tornado? The Velcro hook and loop design was invented by someone who studied the way the burrs stuck to clothing. Heat-seeking Scud missiles were fashioned after the techniques use by rattlesnakes to seek out objects emitting heat.

Another technique designed to uncover similarities is the excursion technique. This technique, designed by George Prince, the creator of the Synectics creative problem-solving process, relies heavily on analogies, metaphors, and mental excursions. Excursions take a person temporarily away from the problem so that she can change her perspective and then relate what she finds on her excursion back to her original problem or situation. According to Prince, the important steps of the excursion technique are as follows:

1. Participants must put the problem out of their minds.

2. The facilitators lead them in the use of some right-brain functions (imaging, connection making, pattern recognition) that are apparently unconnected to the problem.

3. Participants relate the seemingly irrelevant material back to the problem at hand.[5] The excursions might be real (a visit to an air-

port, a grocery store, or a museum) or they might be imagined (playing on a beach, visiting the future, or starring in a movie). Excursions help the subconscious mind to work on the problem to find solutions grounded in seemingly unrelated events or locations.

How to Implement This Creative-Connections Powertool. Spend some time thinking about how the problem, product, process, or program is similar to other situations. Draw analogies to similar situations. For example, what similarities can you find between fast-food restaurants and your organization? What similarities can you find between a baseball team and your team? What similarities can you find between your sales process and eBay's? Relax your mind and try the excursion technique. You might discover a new connection through a very unrelated source!

Creative-Connections Powertool 3: Breaking Down the DNA

Description of This Creative-Connections Powertool. Sometimes the problem or situation is overwhelming in its complexity. A good technique in this case is to break the problem down bit by bit so that the focus is on the "bits" instead of on the whole problem all at once. It is then easier to understand what is driving the problem and identify unique ideas to solve part, if not all, of the problem. Pulling apart a product or service to find the underlying "DNA" elements is easy. Simply list the characteristics or attributes of the product or service and then ask questions or play with each of the elements.

Doing the DNA breakdown is similar to a technique called "reverse engineering." During the Cold War, the National Defense strategy was to capture Soviet spy planes to determine the level of technology that the Soviets were using. The Americans would capture the spy plane and then take it apart to examine the construction of the plane as well as the state of the technology. The process of working backward from the finished product to discover how the object was constructed is called "reverse engineering." Many computer software companies use this technique. They purchase their competitor's product and then pull it apart to see how it was put together. This technique could be used in many other product and service categories as a means of discovering new ideas, or the elements of new ideas.

Pulling apart a process is a little more difficult. For this technique, the team needs to outline the process step by step. At Walt Disney World, for instance, they have done the DNA exercise for their customer service processes and have thought of everything. From the time a customer hears about Disney World, through requesting information, arriving and entering the parking lot, purchasing the tickets, reviewing the maps, lining up for the attractions, boarding the rides, disembarking from the rides, and so on, the staff at Walt Disney World have analyzed every step to ensure that the process flows smoothly.

How to Implement This Creative-Connections Powertool. First, outline all the component parts of the product or all the steps in the process. By looking at the DNA, the team can highlight where the issues and opportunities are and see how to the elements could be changed. For example, they might want to:

- Rearrange steps in the process, such as putting the quality checks at the beginning of the process instead of at the end so that no faulty parts are used throughout the process. This creative idea would reduce downtime and waste. Or as FedEx did, they might rearrange the warehouse locations so the flow of packages is optimized. Their packages might not take the most direct route to the destination, but by stopping in for centralized processing, the overall system is maximized.

- Consider skipping a step, as Michael Dell did when he discovered that computers did not need to be sold through retail stores but could instead be shipped right from the manufacturer to the customer. In doing so, he simplified the process of purchasing a computer, which led to the meteoric rise of the Dell Computer Corporation.

- Add a step. For example, consumers used to just wash their hair. But then the shampoo manufacturers decided that consumers needed to not only wash their hair, but also condition it, as well as add styling gel and hairspray. The same happened with the laundry industry when fabric softener was added. Adding steps to the process might represent creative ways to market new products or services.

Creative-Connections Powertool 2: Listing and Twisting

Description of This Creative-Connections Powertool. Once the steps in the process or attributes of the product or service have been "listed," they can be "twisted" to find new ideas.

How to Implement This Creative-Connections Powertool. Use your imagination and the following chart as stimuli for "twisting" ideas:

Figure 3-2. The list and twist checklist.

Add a step
Eliminate a step
Rearrange the steps
Outsource a step
Add an ingredient
Eliminate an ingredient
Change an ingredient
Combine ingredients
Make it bigger
Make it smaller
Make it more expensive
Make it less expensive
Change the state
Change the shape
Put some fun it
Divide it

Find other uses
Find other customers
Improve the quality
Decrease the quality
Make it easier
Make it more complicated
Align with another product
Align with another service
License
Find new distribution
Substitute materials
Combine other processes
Make it educational
Speed up

Slow down
Add sound
Add motion
Add texture
Change packaging
Automate parts
De-automate parts
Standardize
Accessorize
Make it more extreme
Make it less extreme
Separate
Make it self service
Bundle with others
Make it more reliable
Change color
Automate parts

Creative-Connections Powertool 1: Becoming a Visual Thinker

Description of This Creative-Connections Powertool. Something happens when one gets away from the linear process of listing things and starts to doodle or draw. The subconscious mind takes over and somehow, new connections seem to just appear. That is because many people are visual learners. They learn better by seeing ideas rather than hearing them. As Howard Gardner suggested, some people have highly developed "spatial intelligence." They see relationships between objects or items in a visual sense much more clearly than if they were just seeing a list of items or hearing someone read a list. For such people, a visual depiction of the objects and their interrelationships is needed to make new creative connections.

It is believed that Leonardo da Vinci created an early version of the storyboard technique. Walt Disney perfected this technique to organize his animation projects.[6] By visually displaying the scenes involved in the plot, Disney was able to add, delete, or rearrange them to produce the most entertaining program. Michael Vance built on this technique of displayed thinking by encouraging people to work in color, not black and white, and to work in images, not lists.[7] Advertising agencies use the storyboard technique to visually display the flow of their proposed television advertisements.

Mindmapping, created by Tony Buzan, is another visual creative-connections technique. In brief, it is a visual depiction of the links and connections between thoughts—a form of "structured doodling." This particular non-linear technique helps to generate ideas in a way that, especially when presented in group settings, is less prone to produce biased reactions than are traditional "lists" of ideas. Mindmapping also makes transparent the relationships between ideas and concepts.

How to Implement This Creative-Connections Powertool. Essentially, the mindmapping technique includes beginning with the key issue or challenge in the center of the page, then quickly creating large branches from the key issue that represent ideas pertaining to the issue. From there, more branches are created either from the main issue or from branches that already exist. It is important to branch out freely and quickly so that as many connections as possible are made as quickly as possible. Don't be afraid to be messy! Mindmapping is a valuable tool for showing relationships between elements, demonstrating multiple perspectives, and showing the breadth and depth of a complex issue. There are also many creative-thinking and mindmapping software programs, such as IdeaFisher, Innovation Toolbox, Inspiration, MindManager, Personal Brain, The Brain, and Visual Mind. Information and, in some cases, demonstration versions of these programs, can be obtained on the Internet.

Other visual techniques include drawing relationship maps or interrelationship diagrams, which serve to show the relationships between various causes of the problem as well as enabling one to see the problem in its totality.

Evolving from Brainstorming to Innovation Groups

A chapter on discovering new connections would not be complete without a discussion of brainstorming. Outlined on the following pages is a brief discussion of brainstorming and a recommendation to try an Innovation Group as an alternative.

The Creation of Brainstorming

Advertising executive Alex Osborn created brainstorming in 1938 as a group method for idea generation.[8] It has grown to be one of the most popular methods used by groups all over the world to tap into different participants' perspectives and experiences in order to generate many alternative ideas. Osborn was influential in the design of brainstorming as a process in that he recognized that creativity could be increased by banning evaluation during the idea-generation phase. If the participants were to offer their ideas rapidly, there would not be time to evaluate or debate the ideas. Accordingly, Osborn developed four guidelines for brainstorming: 1) defer judgment, 2) strive for quantity, 3) seek unusual ideas, and 4) combine or build on others' ideas.[9]

The Challenges with Brainstorming

Unfortunately, the application of the original concept and process of brainstorming has been modified over time, resulting in a loss of its effectiveness. The typical brainstorming session now involves a leader who shares some adaptation of the rules of brainstorming, reads the problem statement, asks participants for ideas, organizes the ideas, and then requests that the participants select the best one. The appeal of the original concept of brainstorming has been restrained by the addition of the selection step. The original concept did not include this selection step as it focused strictly on divergent or exploratory thinking.

Although the participants start out with good intentions, there are numerous problems that are usually encountered, in some form or other, with brainstorming as it is now practiced:

1. ***Lack of process.*** Most people view brainstorming as an "event" that is not part of a larger innovation process. The event is often unstructured, no tools are provided, and participants are unsure of what will happen during and after the event. In most instances, the leader reads the problem statement, and then the participants proceed to drain the ideas from their minds. As the event is unplanned, many of the exercises do not relate to the specific challenge at hand. Often the flow of the event is disjointed as participants mix the discussion of the problem with action steps offered at random.

2. ***Lack of a skilled facilitator.*** The facilitator may not understand the overall process or that the facilitator's role should be focused on guiding the process rather than offering ideas. Some facilitators redirect the meeting to fit their personal agendas and sometimes acknowledge only certain ideas, screening out others. These actions have a demotivating effect on the participants and do not fulfill the intent of authentic brainstorming.

3. ***Lack of skilled participants.*** Brainstorming sessions can be disrupted by a few participants who dominate the meeting while the quieter participants withdraw. Some participants view brainstorming sessions as a chance to flaunt their technical knowledge. Other conflicts can surface when managers try to influence the flow of the meeting and subordinates try to offer only ideas they believe their manager wants to hear.

4. ***Listing of rules.*** Often the brainstorming session begins with the leader reading a list of rules of conduct. Unfortunately, reading a list of rules does not guarantee that the participants understand the philosophy behind the rules nor that they will follow them.

5. ***No agreement on the problem.*** Often the focus of the brainstorming session is on identifying solutions for a given problem, when what is

really needed is a dialogue session to clarify and reach a common understanding of the problem or issue. Not enough time is spent on exploring and analyzing the Real Problem. The problem may also be too complex to be dealt with in one group meeting

6. ***Lack of stimuli.*** The most common approach to brainstorming is to gather a group of participants in a room and ask for ideas. The leader is usually positioned beside a blank sheet of flipchart paper, and the participants have blank pieces of paper in front of them. No external stimuli—samples, examples, products, etc.—are available in the meeting room to stimulate idea generation.

7. ***Pressure to be creative on queue.*** Not everyone is creative at the same time of day or in the same style. Not everyone can find creative ideas in an office setting. By scheduling a two-hour brainstorming meeting, the leader is expecting everyone to produce creative ideas within that specific two-hour period.

8. ***Pressure to converge quickly.*** Following the listing of new ideas, participants are asked to quickly choose their "best ideas." This step is difficult to do since the criteria for selection are often unknown or misunderstood. Participants are asked to select the best idea without having time to investigate and reflect on the ideas. Some participants want to avoid a conflictual situation, so they choose the most popular idea, or they revert back to the safest idea or the one closest to what has already been implemented. Others spend more time supporting their own idea and convincing others to accept it, so that the focus on solving the problem most effectively is lost. A major complaint with brainstorming is that ideas that are not immediately perfect are discarded.

9. ***Lack of follow-up.*** Teams can spend many hours and lots of money on brainstorming but they often find that the excitement for ideas generated during the session soon fizzles and the ideas are never implemented. A common criticism of brainstorming is that, of twenty great ideas generated during a meeting, one might get accepted and nineteen are forgotten and never referenced again. Then the team holds another brainstorming meeting a few months later and repeats a similar process, resulting in another "new set" of ideas, of which one is used and the rest

are discarded. The team, in effect, constantly reinvents the wheel, and potentially great ideas are lost in the process.

Innovation Groups

A preferred method for idea generation is holding an "Innovation Group," which, because of its comprehensive and rigorous design, goes beyond the more common brainstorming method. The Innovation Group method addresses the previous list of problems by recommending the following:

1. ***A more complete process.*** One must first determine if the goal of the Innovation Group is exploration (exploratory thinking) or the resolution of a specific problem (both exploratory and concentration thinking). If it is only exploratory, then one group meeting may suffice. If it is to solve a specific problem, then a series of group meetings spread over time may be warranted.

Consider the following process steps: a) pre-work to establish the goals of the process and ask participants to explore the subject area; b) the first group meeting to explore and clarify the problem definition; c) time away to reflect on the chosen problem area and conduct more research; d) a second group meeting to explore the subject area and generate ideas; e) time away to reflect on the ideas and add more ideas; and f) a third group meeting to discuss the ideas and select the "best" ones. This final step can include the group or be done solely by the leader. The tactical details are planned from here.

The two- or three-stage group meeting approach helps address the issue of premature closure. Participants have time to reflect on the output and research the ideas that interest them. Individuals can contribute additional ideas they identified outside the limited time frame of the group meetings. Convergence is easier if participants have this time and the opportunity to discuss the selection criteria in the early stages of the process.

2. ***Addressing the pressure to be creative.*** Using a two- or three-meeting process helps alleviate the pressure to be creative in one meeting and allows more time for research and reflection. Participants can generate ideas according to their personal style. Ideas generated outside the meetings can also be considered.

3. ***Choosing a skilled leader.*** The leader may be the person in charge of the project or may be the person who is best at inspiring and focusing a team of participants. If the leader is also assuming the responsibility of being the facilitator, he must focus on leading the overall process and inspiring the team, and not on directing the content to his preconceived solutions. The role of the leader is to guide the process from start to finish, engage all participants, seek equal participation, challenge the participants to dig deeper for more insights and ideas, and in general, bring a high level of enthusiasm to the project.

4. ***Choosing the best participants.*** Participants are responsible for researching the project area, developing insights and innovative ideas to contribute to the team, bringing a high level of enthusiasm to the project, being open-minded, and encouraging others to identify and accept innovative ideas. The leader may wish to add diversity to the group by inviting a few outsiders—suppliers, customers, and experts—to the group to add perspective.

5. ***Providing guidelines.*** The nine guidelines for an effective Innovation Group are:

- Make sure everyone contributes.
- Clarify the real problem.
- Focus on what is wanted.
- Accept partial ideas enthusiastically.
- Accept unique ideas enthusiastically.
- Seek connections using stimuli and other ideas.
- Be open to others' new ideas.
- Challenge others' ideas.
- Allow passion to rule.

6. ***Clarifying the real problem.*** It is important to spend time exploring the various aspects of the problems before selecting one particular problem to solve. The team should be focused on the problems that, if solved, can deliver the greatest impact to the customer and to the organization.

7. ***Introducing stimuli.*** The more stimuli, the better. Stimuli should be included in the pre-work stages as well as during the meetings. Stimuli could include previously generated ideas, samples, examples, idea worksheets, and output from previous meetings.

8. ***Using the Creative-Connections Powertools.*** Use any or all of these tools to stimulate creative thinking.

9. ***Ensuring follow-up.*** The multi-step Innovation Group ensures that some follow-up will occur. Participants are more inspired to contribute to the process because they understand the process and have faith that their ideas will be heard and reviewed authentically. The capturing of all ideas in an "Idea Bank" for later consideration helps develop the innovation capacity of the group.

PART 2

The SEEDS of strategic thinking

Creativity is the foundation of innovation. It is always exciting to discover new ideas—as witnessed by the recent flood of dot-com enterprises. But the dot-com experience also illustrates that creativity is only one piece of the puzzle. An idea can be creative, but it must also add value.

Strategy is really about connecting creativity with value. A strategic idea is the best or most valuable idea for solving the challenge at hand. While we might have a lot of creative ideas, we must still decide which is the best idea among the many options. Should we go this way or that way? Should we allocate the entire budget to support one program or should we save some for a "rainy day"? Should we merge with the other organization or should we pass on the chance to collaborate? Some people find the task of choosing one option over another easier than others. Of course, the pressure to choose the "right" option increases as the implications of the choice intensify and as resources become tighter.

Strategic thinking is an important component of Innovation Management for several reasons:

- It can be used to strengthen the fundamentals of the business or organization. If the base concept of the program, product, service, or overall organization is weak, layering creative ideas on top of a weak foundation is pointless. This would be analogous to icing a stale cake or painting a car whose engine does not run.

- It can be used to deepen the understanding of what is really causing the problem at hand. Understanding the context in which the problem occurs and analyzing the possible causes of the problem are critical first steps in the innovation process.

- It can be used to strengthen communications with teams within the organization as well as with suppliers, partners, and customers. If the team can clearly articulate its strategic goals, the probability of identifying creative and useful ideas that fit these goals is enhanced.

As Sun Tzu so wisely stated, "a general who wins a battle makes many calculations in his temple before the battle is fought."[1] But who should be involved in strategic thinking—the general alone or the general plus his troops? The old model of strategic thinking involved only the executive team and those people who were believed to possess superior planning skills. This approach elevated strategic thinking to the province of the elite and, in doing so, disregarded the contribution of all others in the organization. The new model involves *everyone*. Frontline employees are closer to the actual day-to-day challenges and have tremendous knowledge and insights regarding where the opportunities for improvement and redirection may lie. If all employees, suppliers, and partners can understand the overall goals of the organization and be on the lookout for new creative and strategic ideas, the power of the organization can be magnified. All employees can participate in strategic thinking by (a) seeing the BIG Picture, (b) looking to the future, and (c) doing the extraordinary!

CHAPTER 4

See the BIG Picture

One of the tools for seeing the BIG picture is the Nine-Step Innovation Process introduced at the beginning of this book. (For a diagram of the complete Nine-Step Innovation Process, please refer to Appendix A). To begin this process, it is important to take some time to truly understand the challenge at hand. This includes gathering information about the challenge from as many different angles as possible. The creative thinking tools and techniques, such as building observation skills, asking probing questions, and seeking diverse stimuli, already introduced in previous chapters, will help in completing this first step of the process: Gathering Information.

It may also be helpful to gather information by looking beyond the specific task and seeing the bigger picture. Often we get so focused on our little tasks, on our piece of the world, that we forget about how our actions will ultimately affect others involved in the same project. We sometimes hear people saying, "I only work in the accounting department. I don't have anything to do with the product." "Why can't the marketing department realize that this is a breakthrough invention?" or "I really don't know what the company is planning for next year." This lack of understanding of how the pieces of the puzzle all fit together results in growing frustrations as well as lost opportunities for innovation.

Seeing the BIG Picture enables you to see why your task is important to achieving the overall goals of the organization, how the whole process flows from start to finish, how other organizations are doing extraordinary things, and above all, how the future marketplace is evolving in order to anticipate your own future challenges and opportunities.

In addition to understanding how everything is related, seeing the BIG picture also involves analyzing the many different angles of your problem. Instead of rushing off to solve what might not be the *real problem*, it is wise to take time to step back and gather as much information as you can about the various dimensions of the problem. Doing this will ensure that you are directing your innovation efforts towards solving the most important problem, or the root causes of the problem, versus wasting effort trying to solve superficial or less pertinent aspects of your problem.

Seeing the BIG Picture also involves setting *Innovation Goalposts* so that your innovation efforts are focused on finding the most strategic ideas to solve your problem. It also involves predetermining *the criteria* that will be used to select the best strategic idea among your many options.

Let's take a look at the various elements of Seeing the BIG Picture.

Systems Thinking

A mechanic could focus on one part of the engine, or he could focus on the interrelationship between all parts of the engine. A doctor could focus on one part of the body such as the heart, or she could look at the bigger picture of what is actually causing the weak heart. A politician could recommend lowering the federal tax rate, but he could also see the bigger picture of how a decrease in the amount of tax collected at the federal level could send rippling effects through all agencies and other jurisdictions. These are examples of how things are interrelated and how a change in one area can affect the rest of the system.

All innovative thinkers should understand the concept of systems thinking. Systems thinking has its roots in the natural world with many of its principles grounded in the fields of biology and ecology. In its simplest form, systems thinking is about looking at the whole entity, not just the parts. Importantly, it is about looking at the relationship between the parts and the whole and understanding the effect that a change on one part will have on the other parts. "A system is a set of components that work together for the overall objective of the whole. Systems thinking is a new way to view and mentally frame what we see in the world . . . whereby we see the entity first as a whole with its fit and relationship to its environment as primary concerns; the parts secondary."[1] Unfortunately, most people have been taught to focus only on the parts of a project or organization that are relevant for the completion of a particular task and, consequently, they only see a small percentage of what is really going on. But in breaking things down into these small parts, they often lose the ability to see how things fit together and cannot identify ideas that could benefit the whole organization.

Systems thinking is important to Innovation Management because it can help everyone:

- To see themselves as part of a larger enterprise with a common purpose. It is helpful to see how the parts of the whole organization (departments, functions, groups) can work together to set project priorities and allocate resources to achieve a common goal.
- To see how one change can affect many other parts of the system. Being a systems thinker means understanding how decisions are being made, how all decisions are interrelated and how, if an organization is to be successful, all decisions link with and support the organization's overall strategic direction.
- To see the world and its opportunities. The world is becoming more connected with the advent of the Internet, enterprise systems, and greater collaboration between suppliers, partners, and even competitors. The more connections one can see and experience through systems thinking, the higher the probability that one can find creative and useful ideas.

Systems thinking does not have to be complicated. Everyone has the capacity to strengthen their systems-thinking abilities. Here's how:

1. ***Look at how your task is related to part of a bigger process.*** For example, list who else is involved in your project from beginning to end, and identify what they are contributing to the completion of the task.

Look at where you fit along this continuum and what you are contributing. Understand what comes *before* your part and what comes *after* your part. This may help eliminate some of the challenges resulting from "just throwing the work over the wall to the next person in the process." Understanding the total process is useful for innovation planning, either to see where process steps can be eliminated or shortened, or to see how new ideas could affect "the way things are done around here."

2. *Look at how your work is related to the bigger organization in which you operate.* Take time to look at how your work relates to that of the rest of your department. Do you know what everyone else in your department does and what projects they are currently working on? Find out what your department's priorities are and how resources are being allocated to meet these priorities. This is an example of seeing the BIG Picture by looking "one level up" from where you are. Take time to also look at how your work and that of your department relates to the rest of the organization. Do you know people in other departments and are you familiar with their work? Find out what your organization's overall business strategy is and how resources are being allocated. Everyone, including research and development personnel, can benefit from understanding the BIG-Picture goals of the organization as well as the steps involved in commercializing a new idea.

3. *Look at how your work is related to the bigger marketplace.* How does your new idea fit with the existing structure of the marketplace? If your idea is for a new product, how will the introduction of the new product affect sales of other products in the company? How will other competitors react to the introduction of your new idea? Expand your viewpoint. See how your product is related to others in the same product category and in other product categories. See what your competitors are doing locally, nationally, and internationally. See who else could be your competitor on a local, national, and international level. If your idea is for a new government program, how will the new program fit with the existing programs in the marketplace? How will other agencies in other jurisdictions react to what you are proposing? Find new perspectives and new ideas by moving from the close-in view to the farther-out, bigger-picture point of view.

4. ***Look at how your work is related to the future view of the marketplace.*** Look at the bigger picture and ask, "How does what I am working on fit with where the marketplace is heading?"

Determine how your current projects or proposed new idea fits with current and emerging customer trends.

5. ***Ask others for their perspective and ideas.*** The world is interrelated, but often people try to solve their challenges by themselves instead of asking for assistance from others who may have faced the same challenge. Is there only one physician who is facing changes in the hospital workplace? Is there only one food manufacturer who is facing the issues of genetically modified foods? Is there only one public servant who is facing budget cutbacks? Although everyone likes to think their situation is unique to them, their team, their organization, or their industry, there are many others in the bigger world who have faced similar challenges. Step 1 of the Innovation Process is *gathering information* about the problem or task at hand. Use the concept of systems thinking to look more broadly at this problem or task. Gather information by asking more probing questions and exploring different perspectives.

Clarifying the Real Problem

"Sales are down 30 percent. We should implement a price discount."

"The competition just launched a cherry-flavored version of their product. How soon can we get a cherry-flavored version of our product out?"

A team may slash its prices when, in actuality, the product's price is not the real cause of the current slump in sales. A team may spend time developing a new cherry-flavored product when the category is already flooded with cherry-flavored products.

Facing pressure to "get a solution out the door," many teams gloss over the problem-clarification step, Step 2 of the Innovation Process, and move quickly into the idea-generation and implementation phases. Often teams spend their time solving insignificant problems that may not even be addressing the Real Problem and which, in fact, add little to the innovative capacity of the organization. The Real Problem may remain and may grow to cause even more problems in the future.

In the previous example, sales may have been down by 30 percent due not to pricing but to a multitude of factors. The problem might have been a low level of service, the poor quality of the product, inadequate distribution, or simply low sales in one particular region. Quickly taking a price discount may lead to a short jump in sales, but it may also just lead to lower profits. The Real Problem of poor service, poor quality, or inadequate distribution would still remain.

If the team believes the problem is pricing, it will work on pricing solutions. If the team believes the problem is service, it will work on service solutions. If the team believes the problem is poor quality of the product, it will work on improving the product. How a team defines a problem determines how it will spend its time solving the problem. A mistake in defining the problem will send the team down the wrong path.

The philosopher John Dewey once said, "A problem well defined is half solved." Spend significantly more time clarifying the Real Problem before you jump to generating ideas or solutions. Here are some down-to-earth tools to help you and your team develop a list of potential problem statements:

1. Rewrite the original problem statement in ten different ways. This will force the team to see more than one angle of the problem.

2. Draw a diagram of the problem. Often the visual depiction of the problem can illustrate the various factors involved in it. For example, if the original problem, in the case of student registrations at a university, was a high incidence of late registrants, an illustration of the communications and registration process might highlight areas where the Real Problem is occurring.

3. List the various *causes* of the problem, not just the symptoms or characteristics of the problem.

4. Look at the problem from a systems-thinking point of view. Look at what might be influencing the problem (the activities *before* the problem occurs and *after* the problem has occurred).

5. Again look at the problem from a systems point of view and list all the elements of the problem from the minor details all the way up to the BIG-Picture perspective.

6. Ask others for their input in order to gain different perspectives. Have everyone on the team contribute their opinions as to the causes of the problem. You may find many divergent points of view or you may find many similar points of view.

7. Use the "YY" creative-thinking questioning technique discussed in Chapter 2 to probe deeper into the problem. Keep asking why until you discover more interesting causes for the problem. One of the most important questions a strategic thinker can ask is the question "why?"

8. Change the assumptions associated with the problem. For example, if the problem is originally stated as "the sales representatives are too slow" or "the sales representatives have inadequate training," change the perspective and explore the problem from the other side, stating it as "the customers are too demanding" or "the customers are too confused." Redefining the problem in this way could lead to a different question, such as "How can the customers serve themselves?" or "How can we educate the customers so they know what to ask for?"

9. Clarify the problem by asking challenging questions, such as the following:

   Who is involved in this problem?

   Who should be involved in this problem?

   What is the level of interest in solving this problem?

   Why haven't we solved the problem before?

   What has been tried before?

   What were the results?

   What has not been tried?

What barriers do we face?

What do we want to change?

What would be the ideal solution?

What rules can be changed?

Will this problem grow to be a larger problem in the future?

What would happen if we ignored this problem?

Once you have had a chance to use these questions for listing alternative problem statements, take time with your team to discuss and choose the most significant ones—the ones that, if solved, would have the greatest impact on the immediate situation as well as on the long-term health of the organization.

Just as seasoned competitors in world-class equestrian events walk the course beforehand and great downhill skiers survey the course before the actual race, innovators need to analyze the terrain in order to fully understand the challenge. Take the time to diagnose the problem before rushing off to find solutions.

Set Innovation Goalposts

Organizational life is full of wasted idea-generation effort. Many such efforts are too random, leading to too many obscure ideas that are not valuable for solving the problem at hand. This makes the challenge of selecting the best idea very difficult, and is one of the reasons why so many brainstorming efforts produce a lot of ideas that are never implemented. In today's fast-paced world where resources are often limited, most teams do not have time to waste on ineffective idea-generation and development processes. What is needed is a more focused and direct approach. Step 3 of the Innovation Process is setting Innovation Goalposts.

Just as hockey players and soccer players need a target area in which to direct their effort, innovators also need a target area in which to direct their idea-generation and development activities. These goalposts effectively guide the development of new ideas by setting limits on the range of ideas that would satisfy the needs of the particular situation.

It is important to note that a goalpost is not one endpoint that players target; instead there are two goalposts between which there is a range of endpoints. How far should the Innovation Goalposts be from each other? The distance between them should not be so great as to confuse the participants by encouraging them to go in too many different directions. Likewise, the distance between the Innovation Goalposts should not be so narrow as to limit new ideas and approaches. There is a balance between being granted too much freedom, which may lead to too many random ideas, and too little freedom or over-direction, which could stifle innovative thinking. The goal of the Innovation Goalposts is focused creativity.

Innovation Goalposts can help the innovation process by:

■ Directing the innovation effort. Goalposts give structure and focus to creative work.

■ Setting expectations. Setting Innovation Goalposts helps participants understand the range of acceptable ideas so that they can direct their efforts toward higher-impact solutions. (This does not mean, of course, that any idea that does not fit within the range should be rejected. Participants should still present a strategic idea that might fall outside the goalposts if it merits review.)

The Innovation Goalposts are designed to help participants understand the strategic direction for the project, the availability of resources, the risk tolerance of their decision makers, and how willing the organization is to accept change. This discussion also helps set more realistic expectations. Many processes wait until the last step to present the chosen idea and gain acceptance. This is too late in the process. Valuable resources have been wasted. If the team waits until the end of the idea-generation and development process to present their ideas, they need to apply extra pressure in order to push the idea through since they have already invested so much time and effort. Many ideas are rejected at the end of the process because they are "not what we were looking for."

■ Facilitating faster decision-making. Just as one would narrow down the choice of vacation locations to one or two viable locations based on preselected vacation criteria, an innovator could narrow her list of solutions based on the preselected Innovation Goalposts.

How to Set Innovation Goalposts

Here's how to set the Innovation Goalposts:

1. Take time to understand the situation by gathering information about the various angles of the problem. Review background information and the context within which the problem is occurring. This may include a review of the business plan, the marketplace, partners' plans, customer needs, technology trends, resource availability, and other important facts.

2. Discuss the various angles of the problem and agree to the Real Problem statement to avoid heading off in too many different directions.

3. Discuss what the ideal solution would look like.

4. Discuss how radical an idea can be and still be acceptable. Discuss whether the team is looking for ideas for Efficiency, Evolutionary, or Revolutionary Innovation.

5. Predetermine the strategic criteria against which the ideas would be judged. This step helps to set expectations of the type of ideas that are wanted and also helps avoid the situation where each member of the team just chooses their "favorite" idea. The criteria will be determined based on the particular challenge, but could include the six *BIG-Picture Criteria* outlined in the following section. These criteria are, in essence, the working principles for developing creative ideas into useful, strategically relevant, ideas.

The BIG-Picture Criteria

In order to turn a creative idea into a strategic one, the idea must solve the Real Problem, and the idea must fit between the Innovation Goalposts. In addition to these requirements, you will want to address the following six BIG Picture-criteria:

1. The big idea must be simple.

2. The idea must support the overall business strategy.

3. The idea must be "distinctly new and better."

4. The idea must be proven.

5. The idea must be profitable.

6. The idea must be quickly and easily implemented.

Instead of waiting to discuss these criteria at the end of your idea-generation and development process, why not use these six BIG-Picture criteria early on in the process to develop your creative ideas into strategic ones and to choose the best ideas among your many options?

The Big Idea Must Be Simple

We can all relate to the many television advertisements whose messages get lost in the clutter because there is no big idea or, if there is, it gets overpowered by complicated humor or entertainment tricks. Great ideas are simple and easy to understand. The more complicated you make the idea, the harder it is for others to understand its greatness.

Unfortunately, being simple is not always that simple. Many people have spent their whole careers complicating things, so moving back to the basics is difficult for them. Some people are even put off by simplicity. They feel that if an idea is simple, it is not worthwhile. This is not the case.

So simplify your idea. Ignore the details until the essence of the idea has been communicated and discussed. Try answering the following statement in one sentence: My simple big idea is ____________________. If you can't explain your idea in simple terms, how do you expect your manager or your customer to understand what you are offering?

The Idea Must Support the Overall Business Strategy

Determine how your idea fits the overall purpose and direction of your immediate project work or the work of your division, business unit, or organization. Show how the idea is compatible with the current and emerging needs of your customers in recognition of the potential trends in your industry. Explain how your idea helps to achieve the overall business strategy. (Of course, you can't answer this unless you know what the overall business strategy is!)

The Idea Must Be "Distinctly New and Better"

Innovation is about introducing something "distinctly new and better" to the marketplace or organization and succeeding in getting the customer to switch from what they are currently using to your new idea. Given the overload of products, services, and programs in the marketplace as well as within organizations, it is necessary to differentiate your offering from those of others. Many new products and services fail because they are not unique and are therefore not needed.

The customer has many options. Managers also have a lot of choices. Why should the manager choose your idea? What is the one thing that makes your idea distinctly new and better than the other options that are available? If you cannot answer the last question, how can you expect your customers or managers to understand what makes your idea better?

Choose one selling point that is relevant and preferred by your target customer. Here are a few examples of organizations that offered distinctly new and better ideas:

- Apple Computers markets colored computers versus the standard beige products that most other companies are offering.
- The Forum Shopping Mall in Singapore offers only children's stores and activities in order to differentiate it from the many other malls in Singapore.
- A tropical island provides the most interesting bicycle tours.
- A beer is unique because it is triple chilled during the brewing process.

If a unique and better element is difficult to identify in your base product or service, try these other approaches:

- The Body Shop markets its unique attitude toward the environment by highlighting its refillable bottles and no-animal-testing program.
- In Mexico, Cemex, the world's third largest cement company promises to provide cement where you want it and when you want

it on two hours notice. Cemex sells promises—not just cement—and uses them as compelling marketplace differentiators.[2]

- Cott Beverages offered retailers low-priced soft drinks and then added value through its consulting advice on how to run a private–label retail program.
- Dell Computer Corporation identified a distinctly new and better process for purchasing personal computers instead of focusing solely on developing unique product features.
- Trimax, now renamed Triversity, was competing head-to-head with other suppliers of retail point-of-sale software systems. Trimax decided to differentiate the market by creating a new, smaller segment in the market called Transactionware, of which it could obviously be the leader. Buyers flocked to its trade show booths to learn about Transactionware while other point-of-sale vendors, who were selling undifferentiated products, looked on.

Some people believe their industry, category, or program is exempt from this concept. They are mistaken. Almost every decision is made by comparing the virtues or benefits of one option to another. Lack of differentiation is the root cause of most strategic challenges. This can lead to commoditization and price discounting. The sales team has to work harder. And it becomes more difficult for the advertising team to develop ads if no one has taken the time to determine what gives the product, service, program, process, agency, organization, or country special status.

Answer the following questions:

- What makes your idea distinctly new and better?
- What is your secret recipe for making your idea unique and able to stand out in the marketplace?
- What do you want your organization to be the expert in or be famous for?

List and then choose one feature or benefit that will differentiate your product, service, or program. Some strategists suggest that you differentiate your product based on benefits—e.g., Tide gives you the whitest clothes—versus features of the product—e.g., Tide has added bleach. However, in today's crowded marketplace, it is best to choose the strongest selling point for the customer, whether that is a feature or a benefit. Choose something that is big enough to be important to the customer, not something insignificant like "our product has blue packaging" or "our product is available in three sizes." Choose something that the customer will understand to be distinctly new and better. A recent television advertisement for Honda communicated the big idea that the car had a Honda engine, which leaves the viewer still wondering "So what? How is the Honda engine distinctly new and better than a Toyota or Nissan engine?"

There is no such thing as a sustainable competitive advantage in today's marketplace. You have to keep moving or you will get run over. Continually re-evaluate your choice of the distinctly new and better feature to ensure that it is still relevant as the marketplace changes.

The Idea Must Be Proven

Unfortunately, people tend not to believe in the potential of a new idea unless someone else, especially someone whom they admire, has already experienced it. Every manager wants to balance the risks associated with new ideas. So show them that your idea has proven potential in the marketplace. Find another organization, either in your industry sector or in another sector, that has succeeded with a similar idea. Or, find examples where parts of your idea have been successful. Even if you feel your idea is new, it will have existed in some other form, in some other market, at some other time. Providing proof that your idea will work, and has worked, will lower the perception of risk. It is also important to be able to prove your new idea to your potential customers. Many ideas fail in the marketplace, not because they were not "distinctly new and better," but because the organizations failed to provide proof of their claims.

Answer the following:

- What is the most important benefit or feature of your simple big idea?
- Why is your simple big idea distinctly new and better than what is already available?

- Prove to me that your simple big idea is distinctly new and better than what is already available.

The Thai restaurant up the street is an example of an organization that, unfortunately, does not understand this concept. Their simple big idea was to offer Thai food in a neighborhood where no other Thai restaurants existed. Unfortunately, their unique benefit of offering good-tasting, authentic Thai food was poorly communicated in the choice of décor. Instead of "transporting customers for a brief trip to Thailand," the restaurant looks more like a cafeteria. There is no visual evidence that the owners of the restaurant know anything about Thai food and, as a result, many potential customers simply walk past the restaurant. Conversely, the waiters at our local Greek restaurant speak Greek, the mural on the wall depicts a Greek fishing village, and Greek music plays in the background. Customers believe that this restaurant provides authentic Greek food.

The Idea Must Be Profitable

Many inventors of new ideas fail to understand the BIG Picture in terms of the whole process of commercialization. They lack the knowledge of how the idea would actually be developed, launched, and maintained in the marketplace, and by doing so, put the acceptance of their ideas at risk. Obviously, any organization has a range of ideas in which they can invest their scarce resources. The decision must be made as to which ideas will be the most profitable for the organization. In order to gain acceptance of your idea, you must be able to show that the investment required to launch and maintain the idea will result in greater returns to the organization than will an investment in another idea.

Assess your idea in terms of the investment required to develop, launch, and maintain the idea. Where will these investment resources come from? What projects will not be funded if resources are shifted to support your idea? What impact will the launch of your idea have on the rest of the organization's portfolio of products, services, or programs?

"Show me the money!" Your idea may be a great idea, but can it make enough to cover the investment costs? How will the organization make money on your idea? What is the revenue model for your idea? How high could the revenue grow? How broad is the customer base? Remember that many large organizations need to attract a big customer base in order to pay for not only the costs of the new idea but also for the organization's overhead costs (costs of administration, executive salaries, office expenses, etc). Ask yourself how your idea could be expanded to attract more revenue (e.g., other new products, new customers, regional expansion)? Remember that many organizations make more revenue by selling "add-ons" or auxiliary products, such as car dealers selling car-repair services in addition to cars, photocopier companies selling toner in addition to the copying machine, and razor companies, such as Gillette, selling replaceable blades in addition to the razor.

The Idea Must Be Quickly and Easily Implemented

Resources are tight. People are busy. As a result, despite requesting innovative ideas, they really want as little disruption to the existing system as possible. They want the adjustment to the new idea to be as easy and quick as possible. Show how easy the implementation will be by highlighting the development and implementation teams, the steps involved, the timing of each of these steps and resource needs for each of the steps. Show how the idea can fit with the organization's core competencies (knowledge and skills) and current processes. Highlight what needs to be changed in order to implement the new idea.

Applying the Six BIG-Picture Criteria

What if, for example, a manager at Starbucks decided to introduce pizza as a menu item for a new source of revenue? Hopefully, the manager would not just present the idea but would consider the six BIG-Picture criteria such as:

The simple idea is selling pizza slices in addition to coffee.

Selling pizza slices supports the overall business strategy because…

Our pizza slices will be "distinctly new and better" in the marketplace because…

Customers will believe we have better pizza slices because…

Selling pizza slices will be profitable. Here are the revenue and cost projections…

Here's how the idea can be quickly and easily implemented…

In this example, we may find that the manager of the Starbucks store will reconsider the value of her creative idea because a) it does not fit the strategic direction of the organization, b) there is no apparent advantage for the customer in buying their pizza slices at Starbucks versus other fast-food establishments such as Pizza Hut, and c) the idea is not easily implemented given the space requirement for additional equipment and the additional labor involved. This is an example of BIG-Picture strategic thinking in action!

CHAPTER 5

Look to the Future

Wayne Gretsky was an exceptional hockey player because he anticipated the future and "skated to where the puck was going." Other less-talented players waste energy trying to catch up to the puck as it is passed from player to player. The same phenomenon appears in many organizations. While a few are looking up and planning for the future health of the organization, many are looking down, cutting costs and managing the day-to-day business. This short-term focus intensifies when people face what they perceive to be "tough times."

Now is the time to invest in building a stronger future, full of hope and exciting new ideas. Looking to the future and identifying strategic new ideas is particularly essential for those countries and organizations that are not blessed with rich resources or low cost structures.

Everyone can benefit from looking beyond what they are doing today to anticipate the future and to develop ideas that will bring stronger results. Some people, of course, do not believe the future can be anticipated. They feel the world is much too random for the making of accurate predictions about the future and that one cannot simply extrapolate the current situation to project an image of the future. While random events can certainly change the course of history, we should not ignore those faint blips on the radar screen that could indicate what the future might hold. For example, there are clear signs that the aging population will require more health care, that fresh water resources are running low, that the mobile phone Internet (m-commerce) era is upon us, that the global economy will flourish, that there will be computer chips in everything, that organizations will employ more and more technology in the pursuit of efficiency and strength in the marketplace, and that there will be more diverse work styles in the future. We should not ignore these signs. The general direction of the marketplace *can* be predicted based on what is happening today.

In order to master "looking to the future," one must develop strong imaginative skills. For some, the concept of imagination is associated only with fictional works such as the recent best-selling Harry Potter series. This view is too limiting. Imagination is indeed an important component of strategic thinking. When combined with a strong innovation-planning process like the Nine-Step Innovation Process, imagination can make the difference between mediocrity and success.

The Nine-Step Innovation Process

The Nine-Step Innovation Process was introduced at the beginning of this book. Unlike other innovation-planning processes that begin with an idea-generation phase, this process is different because it recognizes the need to fully understand the challenge early on in the process. As such, it begins by recommending a thorough understanding of the current situation or challenge, and a discussion of the Innovation Goalposts and BIG-Picture criteria *before* any idea generation takes place. These steps, which have been covered in previous chapters, comprise the first stage of the process, *Understanding*.

This chapter focuses on the second stage of the process. This stage, *Imagination*, involves gathering as many stimuli as possible, in order to maximize the probability of making new connections. With these stimuli and an active imagination, participants are able to uncover new insights. From these insights, new ideas can be identified. The three specific steps in this *Imagination* stage are: 4) seeking stimuli, 5) uncovering insights and 6) identifying ideas.

The third stage, *Action*, involves building the ideas into full business concepts and then into business plans. This stage is covered in Chapter 9. Again, a diagram of the complete Nine-Step Innovation Process can be seen in Appendix A.

Focusing on the Imagination Stage

Let's focus on the steps in the imagination stage: seeking stimuli, uncovering insights, and identifying ideas.

Seeking Stimuli

"Innovation can be systematically managed if one knows where and how to look"[1] Innovators are those people who can zoom out to see a broader view of the world and see new ideas registering on their Innovation Radar Screens before others even know they exist. They stay aware of what is happening behind, in front of, and beside them, knowing that insights can come from any source. Their research antennae are at full mast, looking for signs in the global world of what may be useful in the future.

Relying on only one source of information is like going fishing in a large pond and sitting in only one spot all day, hoping the fish will come to you. What is needed is a bigger hook and movement around the pond. Fish in a larger area than you are accustomed to so that you can see emerging customer needs, technological developments, and trends in the marketplace that could represent new possibilities. Once you have had a look at the information that is available inside your organization, go farther out into the marketplace to discover deeper insights, using techniques such as direct interviews with customers, observation, lead-user research, and benchmarking excellence in other organizations.

Consider the following sources for "seeking stimuli to plan for future events":

- ***Analyzing the current state of your business.*** In order to have a strong knowledge base on which to make future decisions, it is important to research the current state of your business. Consider looking at trended sales information: by geographic region to see which regions are strong or weak, by distribution channel to see which channel is most or least beneficial to the business, by month of the year to see when the business is strong or weak, by customer group to see which groups are most and least important, and by product line to see which line is strong or weak. Compare this information with that of the overall market or industry to see where your particular business is leading or following the market. Look at your revenue, cost, and profit numbers for the last few years to see what activities were or were not effective. Once you have analyzed this information, you can decide whether to build on the business' strengths or allocate resources to address the weaknesses. This decision, of course, must be made in view of the overall trends in the marketplace and emerging customer needs.

■ ***Analyzing current customer needs using the focus-group research method.*** A common approach to gaining insight into customer needs is the focus-group research method. Six to ten people are asked to participate in a round-table discussion in a specially designed room, which is outfitted with a two-way mirror. The client or those interested in hearing the customer feedback sit behind the two-way mirror in a separate room while the participants and moderators are in the main room. The focus-group session usually lasts for two hours, during which the moderator leads the participants through a series of preplanned questions that are designed to tap into their attitudes regarding the chosen subject, product, or service.

Many people use the focus-group research method because they have relied on its use for many years. However, there are several flaws with this method: (a) the artificial setting, (b) the presence of strangers, (c) the lack of time to really probe in-depth attitudes, (d) the lack of real stimuli (opinions are given without the benefit of stimuli such as competitive products and service examples), (e) the assumption that the participants' comments reflect their actual behavior, and (f) the lack of follow-up (any comments or insights the participants may have following the session are lost). Be wary of some focus-group moderators who maintain that their groups are unique because they restrict the number of participants or include creative-thinking exercises. In my opinion, the only difference is that the invoice is higher; the flaws of this technique still remain.

Because of these flaws, the focus-group research method should be restricted to gaining quick insight into what already exists in today's world. Also be aware that you are relying on a group of only six to ten participants to tell you whether your ideas are strong or weak!

■ ***Analyzing current and future customer needs using direct-observation methods.*** Direct observation is a more powerful method of researching customer needs than are focus groups. By going to the source—observing customers—researchers can gain a deeper understanding of customers' true attitudes and behaviors. For example, by watching how customers complete their banking forms, how consumers wash their cars, or how people prepare home-cooked meals, researchers are able to truly see what works, what doesn't work, and what might work in the future.

Direct observation is a powerful method of gaining insight that can then be used to design future products and services. Some organizations have encouraged their customers to join specific online chat rooms. Researchers then observe their conversations to watch for new insights. Other organizations choose to observe the old-fashioned way—by watching how consumers actually behave. "Nissan designers were startled to see how many people were eating in trucks, not just drinks but whole spaghetti dinners."[2] Intuit, the maker of the personal finance software package Quicken, used observation techniques in their recent "Follow Me Home Program." Product developers gained permission from first-time buyers to observe their initial experience with the software in their own homes. Intuit learned a great deal about its product, packaging, documentation, and installation from this exercise.[3] Rowntree, the chocolate manufacturer now owned by Nestlé, discovered through observation that their customers liked to separate their candy-coated chocolates, which are similar to M&M's, by color. This observation led to their famous advertising jingle, "When you eat your Smarties, do you eat the red ones last?"

■ ***Analyzing current and future customer needs using in-depth interviews.*** Consider interviewing your customers one-on-one to gain deeper insight. In order to research a customer's current and future needs, it is important to listen for what the customer says is a problem, hassle, or unmet need. In this regard, ask your customers to complete the following sentence: "I hate it when your product or service ___________________." Alternatively, ask them to complete this sentence: " I wish I had a product or service that could solve my need for ______________."

How can you or your team use direct observation and in-depth interviewing to find new insights for the future?

■ ***Anticipating future customer needs using the lead-user research method.*** The lead-user concept was developed in a formal way by Eric von Hippel, a professor at MIT.[4] The concept is a fairly simple one-gain insight into future needs and potential new products and services by learning from users who have already solved the problem in a unique way. Often these lead users have already developed prototypes or working models of their ideas that could be beneficial in future development work. A simple example of a lead user involves a dog owner who designed a washable cover for the back seat of the car, using Velcro strips to hold it in place. Since no cover was commercially available, the dog owner created her unique solution to address this unmet need. If car manufacturers were able to see this lead user in action, they could design a removable pet cover as an extra feature in their next car or SUV model. Another example of a lead-user group is young computer programmers who have already created new video games, who can be of benefit to software development companies who are looking for ideas for the next wave of video games.

Unfortunately, these lead users rarely show up in focus-group sessions. In order to locate such people, one must dedicate the energy and related resources to go out and find them. This is exactly what Dave Nichol and the Loblaws product development team did. They traveled around the world interviewing leading chefs and small food manufacturers in order to discover unique recipes and techniques for food preparation. Their ability to find these lead users enabled Loblaws to create one of the best retailer food programs in the world.

The lead-user concept has been applied successfully at 3M through its partnership with MIT. Other organizations have invited lead users who were experts in certain applications or who had knowledge of specific aspects of a project to assist them on development projects. Still other organizations have asked lead users to help them review their operations in anticipation of discovering new solutions that might have been missed. The cost of compensating lead users for their ideas is often small compared with the benefit of gaining quick access to unique ideas.

In our fast-paced world, it is beneficial to get in front of the development line by tapping into the expertise of lead users instead of asking for insights from mainstream customers whose preferences might lean toward ideas that have already been introduced into the market. How could your team benefit from using the lead-user research method?

- ***Researching existing solutions within your category.*** Expanding your research net a little wider to look at similar categories of products or services will provide additional food for thought. Somewhere, the seeds of the future have already been planted and may be starting to sprout. Find ideas that have already been introduced in one country and bring them to another country before anyone else thinks of doing so. A team of scientists and physicians might be doing research on a cure for a certain disease while another team halfway around the world has already found the cure. A product that is enjoying great sales in South America might just be entering the Chinese market but have yet to be introduced to the Australian market. This approach is not "stealing" since the ideas are already in the marketplace and are no longer "company secrets." Be careful, of course, to respect other organizations' trademarks, copyrights, and patents.

The future may have already happened in another organization, in another location, in another industry sector, somewhere on the planet. Find out what's hot in your category around the world. Find out how your category is changing. Find out what the latest innovations have been and try to understand *why* they have been successful in other markets. A quick route to innovation is identifying solutions others have already found and then "reverse engineering" or dissecting them to use the parts that would be most helpful to your specific situation.

Are you and your team researching existing categories in order to design your future solution?

■ ***Researching existing solutions outside your category.*** As more and more categories are merging or overlapping, the pressure to understand the dynamics of surrounding categories is mounting. For example, financial institutions can research customer needs for insurance, estate planning, and prepaid funeral services in order to identify new categories in which they might be able to offer new products and services. Food manufacturers can research the vitamin and herbal product categories to anticipate future needs and develop products that overlap these categories. Universities can research the training and development market to anticipate future needs in terms of adult education and online learning. Look at the future for the category next to yours. Do research to find out whether new market segments or new customer segments are emerging.

Innovators have also succeeded by bringing ideas which were "on the fringe" into the mainstream. Blue jeans, athletic shoes, computers, yoga, and tofu are all examples of products that started out on the fringe and have been accepted or are in the process of being accepted into the mainstream market.

Are you and your team researching other categories in order to design your future solution?

■ ***Researching and benchmarking excellence.*** Some people disagree with the concept of benchmarking—looking to other organizations to learn from their successes or failures. "Other peoples' best practices work best in other peoples' companies. Best practices are based on past conditions. The new conditions . . . often cry out for a fresh point of view."[5] I disagree. In today's world, the ability to learn and the ability to quickly apply this learning are the staples for developing strong, competitive organizations.

Why not learn from the experts, both inside and outside of an industry? For example, why not learn about e-commerce from FedEx? Why not learn about customer service from Four Seasons Hotels and Resorts? Why not learn about retail systems from Circuit City? Identify the experts in the particular challenge you are facing and find out how they addressed their similar challenges.

There is a caveat, of course, which is to ensure that the learning is adapted to suit the needs of your particular challenge. You cannot put a car wheel on a bicycle. Different circumstances, different markets, and different times require unique solutions. Attempting to imitate another organization's solutions without careful consideration of the particulars of your own situation is unwise.

Are you and your team benchmarking excellence in others in order to design your own future?

- ***Watching technology.*** Many people are unaware of emerging technology because they are too focused on completing their current project work and have neither the time nor the budget to pay attention to new developments. It is wise to institute a more formal technology watch to find out what technology is emerging, who is producing the technology, and what applications could be derived from this new technology. You will also want to take into consideration technology as it is applied to services, processes, and business models, not just new products.

All innovation is not led directly by customer needs. Often, technology can lead the customer. Did customers ask for a fax machine? Most people did not even know the technology existed until the fax machine was introduced into their lives. Yes, the basic need to communicate was always present, but the desire to communicate in such a manner was driven by the availability of the new fax technology, not by explicit customer demands.

The important lesson, however, is that technology cannot be introduced into the marketplace without consideration of the extent of its appeal to customers. This was the fatal flaw in many of the Silicon Valley start-up companies. They got swept away with the wonders of new technology without considering the breadth of consumer appeal or the strength of the total financial picture.

Are you and your team dedicating resources to watching for new technology and determining the appeal of such new technology?

Trend Watching and Analysis

Trend watching can help you anticipate how the landscape will change and how you can prepare for these changes. Trend watching can help you anticipate what customers might want in the future. For example, car manufacturers could anticipate that as urban centers become more dense, customers might want cars that offer more safety and control. Accordingly, they could begin to design plastic cars that have airbags all around the interior, and of course, brake lights at the front of the car as well as at the back!

Health care providers and hospitals can also predict future demands based on trends. They are facing or will face tremendous changes brought on by new technologies, more demanding patients, budget constraints, the aging population, and regulatory changes. They can anticipate a higher demand for heart operations and artificial organs as the population ages. Education programs for physicians and nurses will need to attract an increasing number of applicants in order to keep up with the service demands as the population ages and consumers continue to demand quality service. Pharmaceutical companies can anticipate that their consumers, the patients, will become more and more demanding regarding access to information on their particular diseases and available treatment options.

Trend watching can also help an organization anticipate what employees might want in the future. For example, younger workers might demand more involvement in decision-making and might rebel against what they see as the bureaucratic nature of some organizations. These employees will be quite vocal with their concerns since they have been conditioned, in most cultures, to voice their opinions since they were young children. Other employees might want more entertainment and excitement in their jobs, expect to have access to the latest technology, and demand more flexible hours and benefits, including childcare.

Many organizations suffer because they plan for the future based on where they have been in the past or where they are today. This is an example of "inside-out thinking." By elevating the needs of the organization above those of the external world, the organization jeopardizes its ability to merge effectively with the changing world. Now more than ever, it is important to see how the conditions of the marketplace are changing. Looking for and seeing patterns in a broader marketplace gives you a jumpstart on preparing the organization for the impact of these trends. Looking at how the marketplace is evolving prevents you from getting hit with a tidal wave of new competitors who are changing your marketplace before you even knew they existed.

It is important to note that not all trends are the same. There are essentially three categories of trends:

1. ***Fads.*** A fad is a craze or a short-term mania for a product, service, or idea. The enthusiasm behind a fad is only temporary and soon starts to disappear. Perhaps it is not coincidence that the word "fad" looks almost like the word "fade." The current interest in bowling shoes as a fashion statement is a short-term fad that may soon lose its appeal. With the world becoming more interconnected, a fad can start in one country and surface in another country within weeks. Fads should not be discounted as unworthy of attention. The Hula Hoop, a plastic ring that you could slip around your waist and twist round and round, sold over 25 million units in 1958 before it lost its appeal.[6]

2. ***Shifts.*** This is the more classic category of trends. Simply put, a shift represents a change in position. In relation to trends, a shift could represent a general change in direction in terms of attitudes or behaviors. For example, there is a shift toward the Internet and away from television as a source of entertainment. There is shift toward an interest in health and wellness and a corresponding interest in natural remedies. There is a shift toward spontaneous expression of personal preferences and a shift away from formal protocols. All these examples represent shifts or general changes in direction. Unlike fads, shifts are easier to see and predict and also have a tendency to last longer.

3. ***Leaps.*** Leaps are giant steps or jumps into the future. While shifts plod along, leaps result in more dramatic changes. Leaps can disturb current practices and cause a dramatic change in direction. Leaps can cause a sudden "dogleg" turn while shifts are on a somewhat more linear path. The telephone, automobile, airplane, Internet, and human genome project all represent leaps in the foundation of knowledge and its application. Unlike shifts, leaps are more difficult to predict.

When you see a trend starting to take shape in the marketplace, determine whether it is a fad, a shift, or a leap, as this classification could help you determine the importance of responding to this trend in your future planning efforts.

For a list of ninety-nine trends to consider as stimuli, refer to Appendix D. Here are a few of those trends for you to consider:

Trends	Explanation
Health consciousness	There is an increased interest in the impact food has on health. Consumers want to know "What is in this?" They desire more information on toxins in their food, air, water, and homes. Patients are asking for new drugs, alternative natural cures, and artificial organs. There is also a growing anti-aging therapy movement.
Higher unemployment	Unemployment is increasing due to technology and dependence on the global market. Machines are replacing the need for employees in some job positions.
Immigration	There is a more global movement, leading to a wider mix of ethnicity and increasing diversity in most regions.
Powerful aging "boomer" population	"Boomers" will demand more products and services for their specialized use. The aging population will splinter into several groups ranging from the young seniors (age 50–65) to mid seniors (65–75) and older seniors (75–100) instead of being addressed as one cohesive "seniors" group.
Rebellion	There is a loss of respect for traditional authority figures. There is a movement toward less formality, protocol, and respect for "the rules." There is more evidence of personal expressions of aggression (road rage, parking lot rage, air rage). There is a growing militant anti-globalization movement. Employees are also rebelling against traditional bureaucratic systems and demanding more participation in decision-making at all levels of the organization.
Safety	Fear leads to greater demand for security–gated communities, car alarms, and martial arts instruction. People want more safety in their homes, offices, schools, malls, and airplanes.
Crisis of purpose	People are busy, but not happy. People are wealthy, but not happy. People are retired, but not happy. They feel empty and lack fulfillment. There is a desire for more fulfillment. This is especially acute for those people struggling with early retirement (age 55) and ways to be productive and fulfilled for the next 25 years of their lives.
Collaboration	There are more alliances and networks where teams from competing organizations collaborate for mutual benefit. The move toward collaboration is shifting the traditional organizational structure.
Speed	Everything must be built for speed. Everyone is impatient and wants immediate service. They demand real-time responses. Speed is not just a competitive advantage; it is a price of entry.

Technology	Computer technology is everywhere. There is growing interest in nanotechnology, the science of the small. Inventors look to put computer chips in everything. Cheap bandwidth leads to greater access and more and more instant information. Long-distance calls via the Internet are becoming more prevalent. The mobile Internet (m-commerce) era is evolving. Distance learning and remote surgery are evolving. The Internet, Intranet, Extranet rule!

In addition to looking at trends in the marketplace yourself, ask others what trends they believe are shaping your industry and why they think these trends are important.

Analyzing trends takes imagination—to see the threats as well as the opportunities that are emerging as a result of the trends. When you see a trend, ask yourself the following five questions:

1. What is causing this trend?
2. How will this trend affect my team and my organization?
3. What problems will this trend cause?
4. What opportunities does this trend offer?
5. How can we turn this trend into a practical application?

Uncovering Insights

"Noticing small changes early helps you adapt to the bigger changes that are to come."[7] Failing to see the changing marketplace, or what Theodore Levitt characterized as "marketing myopia," can lead to serious challenges.[8] "Beginning in the early 1970s, Sears was not noticing or responding to changing shopping habits. These trends included fewer mall visits by two-career families, and importantly, encroachment by aggressive competitors such as . . . discount stores and Home Depot."[9] Failing to see emerging competition and changing consumer habits can seriously impede the future success of any organization. Are universities ready for the new competition from corporate universities and online or distance education providers? Is Hallmark Cards ready for the proliferation of free electronic cards from Internet providers such as Blue Mountain.com? Are department stores ready to combat the increased competition from online retailers?

Insight mining, or translating new information into insights, is both an art and a science. The science part includes the ability to analyze market conditions, consumer needs, and internal circumstances, and then, through experience and judgment, convert this information into insights. The art part includes the ability to be more aware of the opportunities in the marketplace and, through imagination, mold this information into further insights. The ability to see new opportunities—emerging customer needs, new products, services, segments, and markets—as well as the ability to see before others do where superior value can be offered, is critical to building an organization's innovation advantage.

Organize your information and then hold Innovation Groups to turn your stimuli into insights. You will want to combine insights in four key areas: customer needs, emerging technology, the marketplace, and your organization's needs:

1. ***Customer Needs.*** Preselect the customer group you are interested in serving. You may wish to target the most profitable customers, or customers who may be underserved at the moment, or customers who are early adopters of breakthrough products and services. Make a list of their top needs or problems and select those needs or problems you want to solve. Discuss what they are currently using to fill these needs and why they might want to switch to a new method, product, or service. Discuss what is and is not working with their current approach.

For example, IDEO, the design firm, is famous for identifying key customer needs and then directing its collective imagination toward creating new product designs to meet three or four top needs. Note that these needs can be rational or emotional. As the world becomes more overloaded with products and services, the customers' basic needs, such as low price, good quality, and fast service, will become the price of entry in any category. Any product or service that does not meet these basic needs will not even be considered. The arena of competition will shift to meeting customers' more advanced needs in a distinctly new and better way.

2. ***Emerging Technology.*** Next, identify the impact that existing and emerging technology could have on these customer needs. Discuss the various applications of this emerging technology, and then marry these technology insights with your list of customer needs.

3. ***The Marketplace.*** Then, discuss the dynamics of your industry sector or category. Identify how your category is changing. What is the size of the market? How fast and in what direction is it growing?

4. ***Your Organizational Needs.*** Finally, discuss at a BIG-Picture level what would be needed, from an organizational design point of view, to meet these customer needs with the emerging technology and the changing marketplace.

Your insights will come from combining your perceptions of the outside world—your customers' needs, the changing marketplace, and emerging technology—with your inside world—your view of how your organization can change to meet the needs of the outside world.

Identifying Ideas

We have looked at two of the imagination steps in the Innovation Process: seeking stimuli and uncovering insights. Now let's look at turning these insights into ideas that can bring value to the organization. In order to select the most strategic ideas, an organization must first choose a vision or future destination upon which to focus its innovation efforts. Without an understanding of where the organization wants to be in the future, it is very difficult to direct the innovation efforts of everyone in the organization. Once the vision or future *destination* has been determined, it is necessary to choose the optimal direction or *path* to reach this vision. If the members of an organization understand the future destination as well as the path they will take to reach this future destination, it is much easier for them to identify and select innovative *ideas* that fit.

Choose a Vision or Future Destination

In its simplest form, a vision is an image of the future you want to create. Microsoft's business vision has been to be the leading provider of software for personal computers. Lance Armstrong's vision is to be the first to cross the finish line in the Tour de France. Singapore has a vision of building a knowledge-based economy and becoming an important hub in the e-world. Your personal vision might be to reach the top of Mount Everest, live in your dream home, or retire to Tahiti.

By discussing and agreeing upon the answers to the simple questions such as "What do we want to do in the future?" "Who do we want to become?" and "What do we want to be famous for?" a team is choosing its vision or future destination. This destination provides a goal upon which to focus the team's innovation efforts.

It is important to stretch the boundaries and overcome preconceived notions of what is possible and what is not. This often leads to new goals that enable the organization to reach far beyond where it is today. As Walt Disney observed, "If you can dream it, you can do it!"

Some visioning processes begin with a view of today's world and work forward to the future. These processes are built on a methodical investigation of the lessons of the past and the conditions of the present. From here, the team can move forward to design the future based on the past and the present. Other visioning processes ignore the past and the present and begin with imagining what could be in the future if there were no constraints. What process is chosen depends on the team's interest, experience, and situational needs.

Here are ten steps to help you and your team choose a vision or future destination:

1. Take a few minutes to discuss the meaning of setting a vision or future destination. Discuss why the team needs to set this vision so that everyone understands the importance of this exercise.

2. Discuss what the marketplace will look like a few years from now. (The time frame will vary depending on the group and the rate of change in the marketplace: if the group is setting a vision for nanotechnology, the time frame might be a year or two, but if the group is setting a vision for selling cheese, the time frame might be four or five years.) Discuss the marketplace in terms of customers, market segments, and products and services. Also discuss the trends affecting the future marketplace.

3. Identify the key factors that could cause a business or organization to succeed or fail in this future marketplace. Discuss the economics of your particular industry, as well as what the key profit drivers are and could be in your particular industry.

4. Identify how the business or organization could be positioned to take advantage of the future marketplace, trends, and key success factors. What would it take to react to these changes?

5. Ask "What if . . . " questions. Change your view of the customer, product line, service level, competitive set, and marketplace to find new options. Ask "What if the same thing that happened to the music industry with Napster and MP3 also happened to our industry?" "What if a catastrophe similar to mad cow disease happened to our industry?" "What if the customer didn't need us anymore?"

6. Discuss and list alternative views of a future organization. Your team may wish to expand this step to ask as many people as possible in the organization what they see as the future destination of the organization.

7. Choose the preferred vision or future destination based on these previous discussions. Debate whether your organization wants to shake up the industry, be a pioneer and stand out on its own, or whether your organization prefers to follow the mainstream. How radical does the organization want to be? Although stretch goals may be inspiring, they can also cripple an organization if they are not achievable.

8. Identify what your organization wants to be number one in, and what you want to be famous for. What will your unique core competencies (skills, knowledge, and talents) be?

9. Define the vision or future destination in words that have meaning. (Many vision statements are vague and, as such, are not inspiring.)

10. Share this vision widely so that all employees, partners, suppliers, and customers can understand this chosen direction.

Planning the vision or future destination does not have to be complex and time-consuming. Set aside a workshop or offsite meeting to discuss future options with the team. As a case in point, the team at Global Crossing Conferencing recently spent three high-energy days discussing the options for future growth. The process was very simple. The team acknowledged the list of potential uncertainties about the future markets, customer needs, and technology. Despite these uncertainties, the team moved forward to look at various segments of the market and anticipated the growth for each segment, both domestically and internationally. The team noted the list of expected competitors and their respective strengths for each segment, and then they looked at their own growth options and discussed where the optimal segments of the market might be. This discussion was also linked with an analysis of what internal capabilities would need to be considered (processes, skills, resources, research and development) in order to grow in one direction or the other. Various resource materials made the process of discussing and selecting the options easier. They then took time to reflect on the output of this meeting and regrouped to agree upon a collective vision.

Many problems occur when an organization has not taken the time to agree upon its destination. This is like having ten people on a bus with everyone wanting to drive to a different destination, which, obviously, results in wasted time, effort, and, of course, valuable gasoline resources!

Choose the Best Path to Reach Your Future Destination

Once the destination has been selected, the team must discuss and then choose the best path for reaching this destination. Many organizations take a very superficial view of planning. Instead of looking at multiple directions or paths to reach the vision or future destination, they choose only one. If any options are considered, they are usually limited to "low, medium, and high volume and revenue" scenarios based on this one path. How deep is your team's planning process?

In the future, other organizations will be expanding into your territory to tap into your revenue source. Customers' needs will be evolving. Technology will advance. No organization can be prepared for battle overnight. It is wise to spend some time preparing for the future by discussing how each direction or path might play out. "Using alternative scenarios, the future literally becomes a matter of choice, not chance."[10]

Take time to look at the steps needed to make your vision a reality. There are, of course, a multitude of paths that can work in any one environment. Here are five paths for you and your team to consider:

1. ***The cost leadership path*****:** differentiating the organization by providing the lowest cost option in the marketplace. Of course, cost leadership is difficult to achieve in the world market because many other countries and organizations can provide low-cost options.

2. ***The product or service differentiation path*****:** differentiating the organization by providing the most unique products or services available in the marketplace. This uniqueness can be achieved by marketing unique products, branding these products, or holding a specialized patent.

3. ***The customer segmentation path*****:** catering to a unique segment of the market, preferably being the only organization targeting this unique customer segment.

4. ***The superior process path*****:** offering the fastest, highest-quality or most desired customer service in the marketplace. Superior processes can rely on unique technology, superior customer information databases, or offer customers more "power" over the decision-making and purchasing process.

5. ***The superior distribution path*****:** offering the customer a preferred distribution and delivery option such as factory warehouse shopping or global purchasing via the Internet.

Consider using the following chart to discuss the paths your team can take to reach your vision. Discuss and then choose your optimal path based on your own team's criteria, or use the six Big Picture criteria highlighted in Chapter 4: (a) that it be simple and easy to understand, (b) that it support the overall vision or destination, (c) that it is "distinctly new and better" in the marketplace, (d) that it be low risk and can be proven to be low risk, (e) that it be profitable, and (f) that it be quickly and easily implemented.

Our Vision is: ________________________________

To achieve our vision, here are our different paths and how they rate against the criteria:

	Simple, Easy to Understand	Supports the Vision	Distinctly New and Better	Low Risk, Can Be Proven	Profitability	Easy to Implement
Path Option A:						
Path Option B:						
Path Option C:						
Path Option D:						

Ideas for Future Expansion

Once the team has chosen its destination and the most strategic path to reach this destination, it can look for ideas that support this future direction. Here is a list of twenty-four ideas that you and your team can consider for future expansion.

Expand the current portfolio of products and services by:

- ***Reminding current customers*** by advertising your products and services, or by advertising specific benefits or aspects of the product or services of which the customer may be unaware.

- ***Selling more to your current customers*** by offering promotions or volume discounts for a limited time, such as a "buy 2, get 1 free" offer.

- ***Selling more often to your current customers*** by promoting frequent purchases via a loyalty-card campaign. For example, Second Cup Coffee offers a free cup of coffee after ten purchases.

- ***Finding other uses for your product or service.*** Arm and Hammer encouraged consumers to place an open box of baking soda in their refrigerator to mask food odors. The use of Ziploc bags has expanded to include uses other than food storage. Absorbine, once only a remedy for sore muscles in animals, is now available in a less potent formula, Absorbine Junior, for relieving sore muscles in humans.

- ***Finding a new distribution channel*** such as eBay.

- ***Creating a new occasion.*** Hallmark Cards is famous for promoting new holidays in order to encourage higher sales. Cereal manufacturers encourage consumers to eat cereal as a snack in addition to having it for breakfast.

- ***Decreasing the price*** with special events such as back-to-school sales.

- ***Offering various price points*** as hotels do with standard and deluxe suites.

- ***Adding a service to the product*** such as offering free ski wax with the purchase of a new set of skis.

- ***Bundling with other products or services*** such as airfare, hotel, and car rental packages.

Expand to offer new products and services by:

- ***Developing line extensions.*** Disney is a master at expanding the use of its movie properties. *The Lion King* property, for example, included the original movie, video, soundtrack, clothing, books, toys, and even fast-food merchandise.

- ***Introducing new levels of service*** as American Express does with its card programs or as dry cleaning stores do with rush or regular service.

- ***Expanding by offering new services.*** Restaurants are expanding into the rental market where they are offering their premises for rent for cooking lessons, cooking parties, and even executive team training courses where team members can learn to break down their communications barriers by learning to cook together.

- ***Developing new products within the same category.*** Nike, in this regard, recognized the consumers' need for running shoes that were designed for everyday use rather than only for sports and, accordingly, created many fashionable new shoe products. Financial services managers introduce new products and services in order to attract a larger share of each customer's financial expenditures. They refer to this as expanding the "share of wallet." Food manufacturers introduce new products as a means of expanding the "share of stomach."

- ***Developing new products in a new category.*** For products and services operating in so-called "mature categories," it is wise to expand the definition of the category by combining one category with another or by creating a new category. For example, a new category was created in the alcoholic beverage market with the introduction of wine coolers, a wine- and fruit-based beverage. This category can be seen to bridge several other categories—wine, beer, fruit juice, and soft drinks—since the new product could be a substitute for any of these drinks and could draw sales away from any of these traditional categories. Grüv is a new vodka beverage that incorporates gingko biloba, Siberian ginseng, echinacea, and guarana, thus combining the vodka category with the natural-supplements category.

Expand to target new customers by:

- ***Finding new customers for your current products or services.*** Find out what the barriers to using your product or service have been among potential new customers. Decide if these barriers warrant corrective action in order to attract these new customers.

- ***Finding new customers via a new distribution channel*** as Avon and Tupperware did successfully. Vending machines represent a viable distribution channel to target new customers with many products. For example, vending machines in Japan sell candy, soda, computer software, pantyhose, whiskey, audio CD's, batteries, magazines, rice, and videocassettes, to name but a few items.[11]

- ***Finding new customers in new geographic zones.*** Expand your distribution globally.

- ***Redefining the target market.*** Attract new customer groups, such as teens or families. Or do as Tilley, the Canadian hat manufacturer, did when it supplied hats for soldiers who were serving in the United States Army's Desert Storm mission.

- ***Repositioning the product from a niche product to a mainstream product*** to attract a larger customer base. Fish where the fish are. For example, yoga exercise classes have moved into the mainstream, as have products such as sushi and tofu.

- ***Cross selling*** your products to new customers who are already your customers! Financial institutions are learning to sell their loan services to those customers who are holding savings accounts at the same branch.

Expand beyond your current business by:

- ***Selling your knowledge to others.*** Second City, well known for SCTV and comedy shows, has expanded to offer their knowledge through improvisation training courses targeted to business people who want to improve their presentation and communication skills.

- ***Identifying new business concepts.*** Nokia began operations in 1865 as a wood pulp mill. Over time, it changed its focus to chemicals, rubber, and most recently, telecommunications.

- ***Creating new categories and industries.*** Go where no one has gone before.

CHAPTER 6

Do the Extraordinary

In today's world, with more demanding customers, citizens, and employees, "ordinary" is no longer good enough. Once consumers have tasted a better coffee, used a fancier toothbrush, or been served in less than a minute, it is difficult for them to accept what they perceive to be lower-quality products and services. Instead, they are looking for the *extraordinary*, "the exceptional, surprising, and unusually great," as *The Concise Oxford Dictionary* defines it.

In order to help you shift from the ordinary into the *extraordinary*, consider the following nine strategies used by many successful and innovative organizations. These strategies were intentionally developed to be generic so that they could be applied to organizations of all kinds and to workers at all levels—from new recruits to seasoned executives, from free agents to corporate veterans.

Extraordinary Strategy 1: Target the Most Profitable Customer

Should an organization offer products for sale and see which customer groups appear or, conversely, should it preselect a certain customer group and develop only those products that appeal to this group? Classic business strategy suggests that the best route is to target a customer group and develop products to suit the needs of this particular target group, as Gap Kids stores did in developing casual, trendy clothing for children. In reality though, most organizations go back and forth by adjusting their product offering and their target customer groups as the competitive set changes and customer needs and preferences evolve.

However, if you are going to choose one customer group upon which to focus, target the most profitable group. In terms of an existing business, target the top 30 percent most profitable customers, and develop innovative products, services, programs, and processes to suit the needs of this important group. Discuss how vulnerable your company is to losing your customers to your competitor's products or services, and determine the best strategy to continually keep these most profitable customers in your camp. Also discuss why the other 70 percent of your customers are not as profitable. Are there specific activities your team could do to quickly increase the profitability of these other customers without jeopardizing your top 30 percent of customers?

Be on the lookout for new customer groups who could represent significant profit potential. These may be customers who currently use your competitor's products or services, or customers who could be new to the category. For example, mobile phone companies originally targeted affluent and progressive adults but soon expanded their marketing strategies to target a new and very profitable group—teenagers.

The challenge of identifying the most profitable target group for inventors of new products, especially technology products, is a little more difficult. Many inventors dismiss the need to understand the total business picture and prefer instead to just launch the new product and see what happens. This is not the wisest approach since the identification of this target customer group, the size of this group, and the rate of marketplace acceptance are all important factors in determining the resources needed to launch and maintain the new product. Take the time to identify who you are targeting. Everett Rogers categorized the adoption of innovation into five main adopter categories (with the approximate percentage of users in each category): innovators (2.5 percent); early adopters (13.5 percent); early majority (34.0 percent); late majority (34.0 percent); and laggards (16.0 percent).[1] It is interesting to note that Rogers's categorization includes only 16 percent of the population as innovators and early adopters. The remaining 84 percent of the population is waiting for the tried and true. This categorization is important for planning such elements as product design, pricing, distribution channel, and communications strategies to attract the right target group at the right time in the product life cycle.

To target your most profitable customers, ask yourself the following questions:

- Who are the most profitable customers?
- Who will be the most profitable customers in the future?
- What specific needs do they have now and will they have in the future?

Extraordinary Strategy 2: Offer Something Distinctly New and Better

This strategy was discussed in detail in Chapter 4, but it bears repeating. Innovation is about introducing something "distinctly new and better" to the marketplace and succeeding in getting the customer to switch from what they are currently using to the new idea. Remember the fundamental law of decision-making: Almost every decision is made by comparing the virtues or benefits of one option over another.

For example, a person has a choice of over thirty Caribbean Islands to visit. What makes one island more appealing than another as a vacation spot? Conversely, what could the tourism agency for a specific island do to enhance the appeal of their island? What is this specific island famous for? Does the island offer award-winning scuba diving or special landmarks or specialty food or drinks not available elsewhere? What profitable customer group does it want to attract, and how will it meet the needs of this particular group? For example, in the U.S., the tourism bureaus of Hollywood (home of the movie stars), New Orleans (home of Mardi Gras) and South Beach, Florida (home of Latin music) all understand the need to offer something distinctly new and better, so they market the unique aspects of these places.

In another example, how could a hospital fund-raising committee attract more donors? What could they do to communicate that their hospital is the best choice among the many choices donors have?

Become extraordinary by offering something distinctly new and different. Ask yourself the following questions:

- How is this idea distinctly new and better for the customer?
- How does this idea stand out in the marketplace?
- How is this idea distinctly new and better for our organization?

Extraordinary Strategy 3: Set Your Innovation Priorities

Resources are stretched too thin. Everyone has too much to do. But something is wrong when an organization lists eighty-nine priorities for the coming year. Select a few important priorities and focus everyone's efforts and resources toward the achievement of these important priorities.

Selecting priorities is a tough challenge. The team or organization needs to decide:

1. Which products and services to grow, hold or eliminate

2. Which customer groups to support, hold, or ignore

3. Which regions to grow, hold, or eliminate

4. Which projects to support, maintain, or discontinue

In order to do this, they need:

- To acquire information on each product, service, region, customer group, and project;

- To identify the current role that each of these elements plays in terms of its contribution to the competitive strength of the organization;
- To identify the current role that each element plays in terms of its contribution to the overall financial health of the organization;
- To identify the current role that each element plays in terms of the achievement of the future vision.

Resources should then be allocated to support those activities that represent the fastest, most effective route to reaching the future vision.

Depending on how much risk your organization wants to undertake, you should have a mix of priorities, such as:

1. ***A mix of customer groups.*** Depending on the strategy for growth, extraordinary companies might target different customer groups with different products, services, and programs. Credit-card issuers profile their customers into different groups such as revolvers (customers who carry a balance each month and accordingly represent interest revenue for the card issuer) and convenience users (customers who pay their balances each month and accordingly represent little profit for the card issuer). Find out who your most profitable customers are and treat them well.

2. ***A mix of high and low levels of service.*** Many organizations offer different service levels and price these service levels accordingly. The U.S. Passport Office offers faster processing of passport renewals for an extra fee. Other organizations such as restaurants, investment advisors, and airlines offer higher levels of service to their frequent buying customers.

3. ***A mix of current and new distribution channels.*** Experiment with new distribution channels such as the Internet or a new alliance as a means to reach new customers or improve services to current customers.

4. ***A mix of short-term and long-term projects.*** Everyone in the organization should be asked to manage their day-to-day projects alongside several long-term projects. Nokia categorizes its projects into three strategic time perspectives: short-term, medium-term, and long-term.[2]

5. *A mix of efficiency, evolutionary, and revolutionary projects.* You don't want your team focused entirely on efficiency-based initiatives, ones that focus on improving the overall productivity of your current business practices. Make sure your team has a mixture of efficiency projects and projects that represent either evolutionary or revolutionary change in order to position the organization well for the future.

6. *A mix of duplicated projects.* Although this strategy might seem inefficient at first glance, extraordinary organizations like Procter & Gamble and Hewlett-Packard believe in funding seemingly duplicate projects with the belief that the strongest project will survive in the marketplace. "Rather than place its bet exclusively with ink-jet printers or with laser-jet printers, Hewlett-Packard created a completely autonomous organizational unit. It then let the two businesses compete against each other."[3] As Gary Hamel advised, "Somewhere there is a competitor with a bullet with your name on it," so you might as well challenge your own business to find the most innovative way.[4]

Also identify any products or services that are currently seen as low-potential but that could represent significant upside potential. Should these "sleepers" receive a little more attention within the strategic mix?

One of the toughest challenges in setting priorities is identifying the "losers" in the portfolio—products, services, or projects that no longer add significant value and are not needed in order to reach the strategic goals of the organization. Identifying the "losers" is especially difficult in the public sector where, for political reasons among others, old government programs refuse to die, and terminating them is a formidable challenge for policy-makers and public administrators alike. Some organizations continue on with losing projects, like a fly that continually buzzes at the screen window in order to get outside when it would be more beneficial to turn around and fly out the open door. Extraordinary organizations have the ability to discontinue these losing projects so that they can allocate resources to finding more open doors.

In terms of the development of *new projects*, priorities can be set by using Innovation Goalposts and the six BIG-Picture criteria presented in Chapter 4. Once the ideas and concepts are identified, you may wish to categorize these ideas into buckets according to their short-term/long-term feasibility and usefulness.

The team should discuss how many projects it needs in order to ensure that the "idea pipeline" is sufficient for the future. Recognize that only a small percentage of ideas actually progress through the whole process from generation to implementation.

To become extraordinary by setting priorities, ask yourself the following questions:

- Have we identified our product, customer, region, and project-innovation priorities?
- Do we have a mix of priorities in our portfolio in order to manage risk?
- Have we identified a strong innovation pipeline of new product, service, and project ideas for the future?
- Have we identified and discontinued any losing products, services, or projects?

Extraordinary Strategy 4: Make Sure It's Easy

People ideally want life to be easy. Many people have profited from providing easy services that others do not like to do, such as a simple service like barbeque cleaning, superscoopers for cleaning up after dogs, an errand service, or a 1-800 tele-tutor service for school-age children who need assistance with their homework.

Here are several ways to make sure it's easy for your customers as well as your teammates:

1. ***Make it easy to understand.*** A focused message has more impact. As President John F. Kennedy so eloquently stated, "Ask not what your country can do for you, ask what you can do for your country." Citizens understood the message because it was simple. Make it easier for customers or managers to understand what you are offering. Pharmaceutical companies still have a way to go in simplifying their message (brand names, packaging, information) so that their ultimate customers, the patients, not just the physicians, can understand their messages. Computer software manuals are still written for customers who have a strong understanding of technology and the jargon associated with it.

2. ***Make it easy to buy.*** Offer multiple access points. Offer customers access to the products or services via the Internet, 1-800, phone, mail, fax, and in-person options. Simplify the selling or communications process so that the product or service can be easily accessed. Bundle your products and services. Learn from the fast-food industry, which simplified the menu selection by offering "combos" or combinations of menu items.

3. ***Make it easy to use.*** "In some subway cars in Japan, the direction the train is moving in and the name of the next station are highlighted on a map as the train is moving. This is helpful on crowded cars when the view out the window is blocked."[5] Immigration departments in some countries are offering easy-pass services to simplify the border crossing process for frequent travelers. Some are even experimenting with eye-recognition technology to facilitate international travel. Ericsson in Sweden and Nokia in Finland are offering wireless mobile phones that can provide the latest information about movies as well as allowing customers to easily make a wide variety of purchases. The mobile phone will eventually replace the need for a wallet as it can serve as a credit card and identification in addition to providing various communication services.

Try eliminating steps for the customer. AOL simplifies Internet access for new computer users by providing an easy-to-use program.

Become extraordinary by making it easy. Ask yourself the following questions:

- How is your idea (product, service, program, or process) easy to understand?
- How is your idea (product, service, program, or process) easy to buy?
- How is your idea (product, service, program, or process) easy to use?

Extraordinary Strategy 5: Pick Up the Pace

Speed is a competitive advantage. Domino's Pizza knows this, so it promises fast delivery—delivery in thirty minutes or the pizza is free. Software companies know this, so they offer technical support on Sundays rather than expecting customers to wait until Monday. The Saturn Corporation knows this, so it offers predetermined prices on its cars so the customers don't have to waste their valuable time negotiating with car salespeople.

"The early bird catches the worm." Unfortunately, for many organizations, the way they operate does not match the speed of the new, chaotic technological world. Much time is wasted waiting—waiting for parts, waiting for information, waiting for approvals, or waiting for others to complete their tasks.

Your process could represent your point of difference in the marketplace; it could be the "distinctly new and better" idea you are looking for. Here are some ideas:

1. ***Eliminate unnecessary steps in your processes.*** Wal-Mart has been investigating the shipment of products directly from the manufacturer to their stores so they can bypass their costly warehouses. Internet companies offer direct manufacturer-to-buyer purchasing for cars, appliances, computers, clothing, and much more. Other organizations eliminate process steps by asking their customers to perform the steps themselves. Customers now access their own money at automatic teller machines, pour their own drinks at fast-food restaurants, and scan their own books at the checkout at the local library. To identify unnecessary steps in your process, first map the process by identifying the activities, information, and people involved at each step along the way. Look for a dysfunctional flow of products or information. Look at every process—upstream and downstream—to find innovative ways to eliminate unnecessary steps.

2. ***Find the bottlenecks in your processes.*** Norfolk General Hospital mapped the x-ray process and found bottlenecks and inefficiencies. The improved process reduced the time it takes for x-rays by 81 percent.[6] Remember, improvements cannot be made in isolation. Even if an organization such as a pharmaceutical company improves its research and development process to save twelve months of development time, the time saved might be canceled out by not having their documentation ready for the government's drug-approval procedures later on in the process.

3. ***Implement seamless processes.*** How often do your customers hear, "We don't handle that in this department. You'll have to call this other number." Coordinate processes from department to department by letting "the one hand know what the other one is doing." Systemize repetitive processes using superior planning processes such as those offered by Emmperative.com. Also consider replacing sequential processes (where Step 2 cannot begin until Step 1 is completed) with parallel processes (where Steps 1 and 2 are done concurrently).

While the efficiency of internal processes is important to innovation, the largest benefit can usually be derived from improving processes with customers, partners, suppliers, and other external stakeholder groups. Supply-chain management, e-procurement, lean logistics, enterprise-resource planning, and customer-relationship management are all areas of growing interest for managers who want to identify more innovative process designs.

4. ***Simplify decision-making.*** Redesign your processes so that information flows quickly and decisions can be made quickly. Streamline processes so that customers can deal with a person who can make an immediate decision for them. Improve the responsiveness of your organization by enabling more decisions to be made by junior staff members. Eliminate multi-layered approval processes for micro items. And remember, your organization is wasting time if your employees are afraid to discuss a new idea and ask questions early on in the idea-development process and are instead waiting until later when they have a fully developed idea.

5. ***Have everyone identify the sacred traditions that no longer add value.*** Cut out redundancy or wasted effort. Have everyone identify "those crazy things we do" that waste time, money, and effort. Identify quick improvements or just eliminate the thing that is not adding value.

6. ***Take advantage of technology.*** Car manufacturers use computer simulation to design key platform components in order to save time and money in the development process.[7] Technology enables them to experiment with different concepts and to "fail fast." Use technology to maximize the flexibility of your product or service. Most hotels and motels now use technology to provide up-to-date information on their room rates. A digital sign on highway I-75 in Michigan, for example, advertised the latest room rate at the Best Western as $79. Best Western could easily and quickly change the digital sign to advertise room rates as $49 if they had extra rooms available after 6 P.M. You can also use technology to enhance communications and collaboration with other team members so that time is not wasted.

7. *Operate on customer hours.* With technology and the shift to global operations, many organizations are investigating ways in which they can offer their products and services anytime, anywhere. Brokerage services operate twenty-four hours a day so customers can place a stock trade in the middle of the night. Pizza delivery services and pharmacies are open twenty-four hours. Why aren't dry-cleaners and car repair shops also open twenty-four hours a day?

Become extraordinary by picking up the pace. Ask yourself the following questions:

- How can we eliminate unnecessary activities or "the crazy things we do" so that resources can be funneled toward more innovative activities?
- How can we simplify decision-making so those innovative ideas can make it through the system quickly?
- How can we take advantage of technology to quickly deliver something "distinctly new and better" to the customer?

Extraordinary Strategy 6: Systemize with Modules

Simply stated, a module is a standardized part. By moving to standardized parts, an organization can eliminate the wasted time and effort spent "reinventing the wheel" each time that part is needed. When an organization develops a standard operation or system that is repeated time after time, it can capitalize on the following benefits:

1. ***Customers have a greater sense of power in the buying process.*** Consumers can mix and match the component parts depending on their unique needs. Dell encourages its customers to build their own computers using an array of standardized parts.

2. ***Greater efficiency in operations can be achieved.*** Hewlett-Packard uses standardized component parts for its printers. Starbucks uses a standardized "shot of espresso" in numerous coffee-drink recipes.

3. ***Credibility is increased.*** By using module parts behind the scene, the ability to deliver a consistent product or service to a customer is strengthened. As a result, the customer believes that the organization "knows what it is doing."

4. ***Expansion plans are also easier.*** By having the core architecture in place, researchers are able to identify new products, applications, and improvements more easily. 3M has the Post-it note architecture in place and now just needs to identify more new products that can take advantage of this format. In the automobile industry, where design costs and the need for new car models are high, manufacturers use components that can be incorporated in more than one car model. The time to develop new models can also be shortened if a series of products is considered and multi-year expansion plans are developed.

5. ***Internal processes are easily coordinated.*** For example, a sales team can use the same component parts to produce a standardized sales presentation or internal documents.

To become extraordinary by systemizing with modules, ask yourself the following questions:

- How can we use the concept of modules to simplify our customers' buying process?
- How can we modularize our internal processes?
- How can we use the concept of modules for our future plans?

Extraordinary Strategy 7: Profit from the Power of Branding

Club Med, Viagra, Harlequin, CNN, AOL, Gap, Canada, the Cannes Film Festival, British Airways, Singapore, Motorola, Intel, Marlboro, Tahiti, the Olympics, KFC, MasterCard—everywhere we turn, brands are being offered. Tom Peters even suggested that people brand themselves—with a distinct name, features, and positioning in the marketplace.[8]

A brand goes beyond the simple features of the product to create a distinct image. For example, a cup of black coffee is only a cup of coffee, but by placing the Folgers brand name on it, we have the perception that the cup of black coffee is of higher quality. Likewise, sport shoes with the brand name Nike and women's handbags with the brand name Coach command higher prices than similar products with less respected brand names. So do brands such as Calvin Klein clothes, Diesel jeans, Harley-Davidson motorcycles, and Heineken beer.

Why is branding important to innovators? Here are a few reasons:

1. ***Branding helps break through the clutter.*** Distinct branding helps a brand to stand out in a marketplace overwhelmed by many similar products, services, and programs.

2. ***Branding helps simplify the message and makes the buying decision easier.*** Read these numbers: 3349 192233 456777. Now repeat them from memory. You might find this hard to do. If, however, the message is simplified to 3349, you can read and repeat this message more easily. That's how branding can simplify the message for busy consumers. Most customers are busy and have a lot on their minds. Branding helps facilitate the speed of their buying decisions. They can rely on the most popular brand or continually purchase the brand upon which they have come to rely. A brand name reserves a spot in the customer's memory bank.

3. ***Branding delivers economies of scale.*** Consistent branding simplifies the task of communicating the features and benefits of the product or service. Consumers know what brand to ask for, simplifying the task even further. Similar branding can also be used across the global marketplace, leading to lower marketing costs. "Pursuing a global branding strategy, Nokia has systematically used its brand name across

many countries like brand leaders such as Sony, Nike, Coca-Cola, and Microsoft."[9]

4. *Branding delivers a guarantee of consistency if done right.* You know what Coca-Cola will taste like. You know how solid a Volvo car will be. You know that Four Seasons Hotels and Resorts will take special care of you. The customer knows what to expect from the brand, even from one country to another.

Done well, branding can help not just a product or service, but also a new program. For example, a government agency can benefit from branding its programs so that constituents understand the differences between programs, know what program to request, and also realize the breadth of distinct programs offered through this specific agency.

Branding is not just the domain of the executive team or the marketing team. More and more human resources and operations managers are adopting the principles of branding in order to improve the communications of their programs, both within and outside of the organization. Among other things, organizations are turning to stronger branding programs so that they can position themselves in the best light when recruiting new talent.

Become extraordinary by profiting from the power of branding. Ask yourself the following questions:

- How can we use the power of branding to simplify our selling message?
- How can we use the power of branding to increase the consistency of our selling message?
- How can we use the power of branding to position our new programs to the employees in our organization?

Extraordinary Strategy 8: Add Credibility

If it is difficult to communicate how your innovative idea is "distinctly new and better," you may want to consider adding credibility or prestige from several of the following sources:

1. Investigate the potential of patenting the idea and, if the patent is granted, tell everyone.
2. Win a prestigious award. Films that win at the Cannes Film Festival have instant credibility.
3. Have a leading authority support your idea. Restaurants rely on restaurant critics to write wonderful reviews, writers covet Oprah Winfrey's endorsement, and toothpaste manufacturers pursue the endorsement of the Dental Association.
4. Profile testimonials from satisfied customers.
5. Seek testimonials from celebrities (but only seek testimonials in fields in which the celebrities have expertise).
6. Reference experience in the field such as twenty-five years in business, president of this or that, or author of seventeen books.
7. Advertise that you are "number one" in something or that you are widely accepted by many customers, such as "top-rated movie," "number one in the category," or "have served over nine million customers."
8. Offer a money-back guarantee to lower the risk of trying your new product or service.
9. Offer a sample of the product or service. AOL encouraged people to sample their service with free CD's. Cable channels offer thirty-day trial periods with the hope that their customers will "get hooked" on the new channels. Food companies offer samples of their new food products.
10. Offer insight that no one else has. Highlight the ten secrets or "inside scoop" in your area of expertise.
11. Advertise that the new idea was requested by a large number of customers such as "by popular demand, the product is finally available in Canada."

Become extraordinary by adding credibility. Ask yourself the following questions:

- How can we add prestige by winning an award?
- How can we gain support from leading authorities in our field?
- How could we enable potential customers to test this product or service?

Extraordinary Strategy 9: Create Magnetworks

The value chain has evolved into a value network. It is critical that organizations look for alternative methods to deliver differentiated products, services, and programs in the most cost-effective and speedy manner possible. These methods can consist of different combinations of people, organizations, skills, tasks, and resources, which are assembled on a temporary or permanent basis, depending on the needs of the project. It is important to note that the evolution toward a networked style represents an overall shift in organizational life from centralized command and control to a more participatory, shared leadership style, in which skill, experience, and ideas rule. Here are some ideas on how you can network and involve others:

1. ***Network within your organization.*** First and foremost, remember that opportunities for innovation lie within your organization. Break down your "Berlin Walls" and inspire others to share their insights, ideas, resources, and learning in order to tap into your organization's collective wisdom. Share your work. Make it easy on your team members by sharing your processes with them so they can understand what you do and offer assistance if needed. One organization I worked with faced a production crisis when the person who was in charge of ordering raw materials was involved in a car accident and, unfortunately, was unable to work for several weeks. Since no one understood her process for keeping track of the inventory, no one bothered to order more supplies. The production facility soon experienced an out-of-stock crisis and had to close operations until new raw materials arrived. The warehouses and retail stores soon ran out of stock. Her lack of coordination with her teammates, as well as management's apparent lack of the foresight to employ cross-training, caused a significant financial problem and great difficulty for the organization.

2. *Network to learn from others.* The Internet has enabled many to exchange insights and ideas through chat rooms and shared-interest Web sites. Others share best practices through industry associations or through direct experiences, as the Postal Service of Canada did in an exchange with its Indonesian counterpart. The fastest route to understanding is to network with an entity that has faced a challenge similar to yours.

3. *Network to share the infrastructure burden with other competitors.* Packaged-goods companies, e.g., Coca-Cola and Kellogg's, are looking at using the same distribution resources to take advantage of shared economies of scale. The Star Alliance, a network of several airlines, shares both marketing power and infrastructure capacity.

4. *Network to share research and development insights and responsibilities.* Software companies such as Microsoft encourage users to beta-test their new software programs before they are offered to the public at large. Linux attracted a large number of programmers who contributed their ideas for the development of its new "open source" operating system. Bluetooth, a development project investigating the feasibility of a radio-based link between different electronic devices, is another example of a network or "virtual community of program developers." Bluetooth represents a significant leap forward in technology. Partner organizations include 3Com, Ericsson, Intel, Lucent Technologies, IBM, Microsoft, Motorola, Nokia, Philips, Toshiba, and Texas Instruments. The network now has over 2,000 active members. "When Ericsson, IBM, Intel, Nokia and Toshiba formed the Bluetooth alliance in 1997, they did not just create a forum to enhance the Bluetooth specifications and provide a vehicle for interoperability testing. They were also diversifying risk while ensuring extensive development activities."[10]

5. *Network to outsource.* Outsource the parts of the process that are inefficient for your organization and then concentrate on developing your capacity in the areas that are important to your future vision. Dell chose to outsource its manufacturing. FedEx chose to outsource some of its ground transportation so that it could concentrate its efforts on building a brand as well as a strong technology infrastructure for e-commerce. Some organizations outsource administrative tasks, such as payroll and sales functions. IKEA, the furniture manufacturer and retailer, even outsources to customers, who have the responsibility for assembling their own furniture products. Outsourcing enables an organization to take advantage of "best-in-breed" partnerships and quicker delivery times.

6. *Network to enhance buying or selling power.* Convenience stores network to benefit from strengthened buying power. AARP negotiates price discounts and special offers for its members. Amazon.com and Toys R Us established a service network so they could both benefit by selling toys online, a feat e-toys.com tried to do solo and failed.

7. *Network to create an organization of managed companies.* Four Seasons Hotels and Resorts and Fed Ex are two examples of organizations that oversee the operations of other organizations within their networks.

8. *Network to provide a hub or meeting place for others.* Monster.com, an employment Web site, eBay, an Internet auction site, and the various stock exchanges around the world represent examples of networks established to provide a meeting place for buyers and sellers.

These are all examples of "magnetworks" ("magnet" + "network"), networks of competing and collaborating individuals or teams who innovate together for mutual benefit. The members of this network assist one another in achieving mutual innovation goals. Success breeds success. The stronger the success of the network, the more it attracts new innovation teams, which adds further momentum to the magnetwork. Hollywood (film) and Silicon Valley (technology) are examples of successful magnetworks. Become extraordinary by creating a magnetwork. Ask yourself:

- How strong are our networks within our organization?
- How can we network with other organizations to identify and develop new ideas?
- How can we use technology to strengthen our magnetworks?

PART 3

The SEEDS of transformational thinking

Innovation is a transformational challenge as well as a creative and strategic one. With all due respect to Dr. Deming and the quality movement, innovation is not about statistical process control—it is about flexibility and human interaction. Although it is important to understand the dynamics of creative thinking and strategic thinking, it is equally important to understand how the "human side" of innovation can affect the outcome of any innovative effort. By understanding and attending to the personal dynamics behind identifying ideas and gathering support for these ideas, the probability of actually implementing them can be improved.

There are two categories of innovation that should be distinguished: (1) the business or operating strategy (the actual innovative ideas) and (2) the organizational design (the environment or culture for innovation, including the transformational skills of employees). The focus in many organizations is most often skewed toward finding innovative ideas while the environment or organizational design for systematically finding, developing, and implementing these ideas is overlooked. What is needed is a holistic view of both the business strategy *and* the development of the organizational environment for innovation.

The next three chapters focus on the seeds of transformational thinking: seek greater awareness, ignite passion, and take action.

CHAPTER 7

Seek Greater Awareness

Innovation can be the driving force that aligns your organization. But innovation does not just happen; it needs a fertile environment in which to grow. Transformational thinking is about transforming how we approach our work, both individually and collectively. The first step in transformational thinking is increasing your awareness and understanding of your own attitudes, as well as those of your teammates.

Seek Greater Awareness of Self

Peter Senge, author of *The Fifth Discipline,* introduced us to "The Parable of the Boiled Frog." This parable suggests that if you put a frog in boiling water, it will jump out; but if you put it in cold water and gradually turn up the heat, it will let itself be slowly boiled to death because it is not aware of its surroundings and therefore doesn't perceive any immediate danger.[1] Like the frog, we can benefit from greater awareness of ourselves and our surroundings to enable us to capitalize on more opportunities for innovation.

To be a great innovation leader, you must first be aware of yourself. In order to gain this greater awareness of self, begin with these three easy steps: (1) slow down your mind, (2) calm your mind, and (3) clear your mind.

1. ***Slow Down Your Mind.*** There is no doubt that the pace of work will increase as more and more networks, both technical and social, are formed and set in motion throughout the world. Competition will increase, and many organizations will be forced to shut their doors because they can't keep pace with the demands of the new highly connected world. Work will move to 24/7 with laptop computers, PalmPilots, mobile phones, and e-mail.

As a result of this environment, you find yourself rushing from phone call to phone call, from meeting to meeting. You find yourself responding to people who want everything done in "McDonald's time"—ready in under two minutes.

But how will slowing down help? As most golfers know, you have to slow down the swing in order to see how to correct it. Slowing down the pace can help you observe more and, in doing so, see new approaches or ideas. The 3M Corporation is well known for encouraging its employees to slow down the pace and allocate up to 15 percent of their time to exploring new territory and experimenting with new ideas. By slowing down long enough to notice things they might not have seen before, they have a greater chance of finding breakthrough ideas.

By slowing down, you can also take time to recharge. Even Formula One car engines need to slow down and rest every once in a while to avoid overheating.

2. ***Calm Your Mind.*** Zen Buddhists refer to the distracted, busy mind as the "monkey mind," which conjures up images of a wild monkey swinging recklessly from vine to vine. The mind is like a wild monkey, rushing from thought to thought, facing too many distractions, and not having enough time to really think about where it is going or what it is trying to accomplish. With no time to reflect, the mind swings wildly from task to task, wasting precious resources. Is your mind like a wild monkey mind?

Innovators find their own ways to stop and calm their minds, including creating environments where they can relax and reflect. Most of the creative-thinking research suggests that creativity comes from a relaxed state. While a few people find that they are creative in high-intensity situations or in environments charged with stimuli (toys, music, noise), most people find that their creativity flourishes when they are more relaxed and in more peaceful environments.

3. ***Clear Your Mind.*** Increasing self-awareness also requires that we rid our mind of excess baggage that may be preventing us from thinking clearly. The mind is often cluttered with facts and figures and illusions of the way the world was at some point in the past, or perhaps the way we want to believe the world should be. We all know people who hold onto ideas that are outdated and no longer fit the new circumstances.

Cluttered minds leave no room for new ideas. The source of power for innovative ideas is a clear mind. In other words, a mind must first be cleared of its illusions so that there is room for new and more important ideas to take its place. Try clearing your mind by asking probing questions and challenging your sacred traditions. The more quickly you can discard your old ideas, the sooner your mind can fill with new ones.

Awareness of Our Fears

Most of our barriers to innovative thought and action are self-imposed. Remember the story of the elephant that, at a young age, was confined to a certain spot by a very strong chain. He learned to move only a few feet in any direction. Even though the elephant grew to a very large size with corresponding strength, and even though he could easily have pulled the chain from its roots in the ground, he did not. Instead, he still moved only a few feet in any direction. He had learned at an early age not to test the strength of the chain and simply stopped trying. His ability to find new solutions was limited by his fears.

Are you addressing the following common fears?

1. ***Fear of the unknown.*** Like the elephant, we stop trying new things. However, innovative thinking is about venturing into the unknown. Every time you do something you haven't done before—riding a bike, transferring to a new school, enrolling in a university, starting a new job, getting married—you are building the ability to conquer your fear of the unknown. Remember that, in order to swim, you must let go of the side of the pool!

2. ***Fear of losing what I have.*** People want to retain control. They have struggled hard to achieve their goals—status, power, and money. Why should they share them with anyone else? "If I share my idea with others, might they try to take credit for it?" "If it took me fifty years to get a seat at the boardroom table, why should I invite others with less invested to share in the decision-making?" However, a wise person once said, "You have to go down the mountain in order to climb the next mountain." Sometimes giving away or sharing what we have achieved makes room for future achievements, both ours and others.

3. ***Fear of what others might think.*** Many people hide their new ideas for fear that others might judge them too harshly and potentially reject them from the group. Insecurities prevent people from asking questions and offering new insights. This might be due partially to a cultural upbringing in which some people were taught to suppress their ideas if they did not mirror those of parents, teachers, or managers. However, it is important to recognize that in the field of innovative thinking, having a different idea can be very valuable for the group, and may even represent the breakthrough the group has been looking for.

4. ***Fear of what you might think.*** We all have what Michael Ray referred to as "the Voice of Judgement."[2] Before our ideas even have a chance to see the light of day or to be reviewed by others, we allow our ego to extinguish them. However, for innovative thinking, we need to tap into and trust our own judgment, both our cognitive judgment and our intuition. Intuition is trusting in those things we cannot see but that we somehow "know" we hold true. Many people overrule their "gut feeling" or intuition because they cannot explain or quantify it. Yet, as we know, not all things in life can be explained or quantified.

Overcome these four fears and push the boundaries of your self-awareness. Deepen your understanding of what is happening around you and why it is happening.

There is a difference between empowered employees and those who have achieved true personal mastery. Empowerment often starts outside the individual, as in the case where someone is given license to do something, while self-mastery starts and is cultivated within. One of the elements of achieving self-mastery is recognizing that you have the power to make choices and that, in doing so, you must accept the responsibility of making such decisions. In the moment of self-awareness, great wisdom will appear.

Seek Greater Awareness of the Team

Innovation champions are people who are capable of unleashing the innovative spirit in themselves as well as in others to bring out the best innovative thinking. These are people who can inspire themselves and others to create a climate for innovation, which is really a climate for positive change. To become innovation champions, we must acknowledge the potential barriers to team innovation:

1. ***Being unaware of the effect your attitude has on others.*** Achieving greater awareness means that you are more aware of yourself and others, but also of the interaction between the two. In this connection, it is important to look at how your thoughts and actions affect others. Are you contributing to the development of an open, high-energy, innovative culture or are you draining your own and others' energy by complaining about cutbacks, circumstances which have changed, or difficult people? Spending too much time blaming others or arguing over small issues can drain the energy needed to find new approaches and ideas.

2. ***Being unaware of the increasing need for more developed social skills.*** As organizational structures evolve from the traditional hierarchical style to a more integrated "networked" approach, social skills, or the ability to connect with one another, will become even more important. The ability to discuss and share ideas and then implement these ideas is an important component of team innovation.

3. ***Being unaware of the need for widespread participation in the innovation initiative.*** The days of command and control, of "we are the

powerful and you are the little people," are vanishing. Work is moving toward a more participatory style with recognition that everyone plays an important role on the organization team and that, without the participation of the full team, the value delivered to the end "customer" will suffer. An innovative organization needs the full participation of innovation teams and innovation champions at all levels.

4. ***Being unaware of the team's resistance to change.*** The team, or some members of it, may be too busy preserving the current system. The pressure to conform and agree with the team can prevent the penetration of any new ideas. Even one person can sabotage the innovation efforts of the team. As in rowing, if one person is out of sync with the rest of the rowers, progress is very difficult. A critical component of innovation is the willingness to change as a team.

In order to overcome these potential barriers to team innovation, you need to increase your awareness of your effect on others and strive to develop social as well as technical knowledge skills. In addition, it would be valuable to increase awareness of the need for widespread participation in the innovation initiative.

Begin by encouraging everyone to believe in the power of the team concept. If people don't want to work together, it doesn't matter how strong their ideas are, they will still fail. First and foremost, an innovation team must be made up of people who believe and trust in the value of the team concept. Debra Amidon suggests that the "collective insights of a team produce something far beyond what any combination of individuals might otherwise have created."[3] A good friend and colleague, Ketan Lakhani, who hails from South Africa, introduced me to the transformational management concept of *ubuntu ngumuntu ngabantu* or *ubuntu*, for short, which loosely translated from the Zulu means, "You are only a person through other people." In other cultures, this might be translated as "No man is an island." Without others, our innovation results would be negligible. As John Kao said so eloquently in his book *Jamming*, innovating with a team is analogous to a jazz group whose members alone can make music but together can produce great music![4] The recognition of this reliance on each other is the starting point for forming a strong innovation team.

It is also important to increase your awareness of your team's resistance to change and the behavior that might be limiting the potential of the team. In order to become an effective innovation team, it is often necessary for everyone on the team to experience "confession." Simply put, each member of the team must be willing to admit—or own up to—behavior(s) that may be holding the team back from reaching its highest innovation potential. For example, are you secretly stockpiling excess funds in your budget in order to protect your own interests ahead of those of other members of the team or of other teams within the organization? Are you spending too much time trying to transfer your expenses to someone else's budget? Are you exercising too much control over the little details? Are you killing the innovative spirit in others by changing direction too many times or, conversely, refusing to let go?

Finally, it is important to support diverse thinking styles. Designing an innovation team does not require each member to possess similar values and characteristics. For innovation, you do not want everything to be the same. Instead, you want to nurture the differences among members and invite others to share their diverse views. An innovation community welcomes the diverse thinking styles of each member and seeks to leverage these unique perspectives for the good of the community and its members. Innovation communities recognize that diversity is important for growth and development, so if diversity is not evident, they seek to add it. Every member contributes a different piece to the collective puzzle.

Building an effective innovation team in this regard requires accepting conflicting viewpoints. Creative tension is actually the catalyst for discussing and identifying better solutions.

Team Structures

There is a wide variety of team structures that can be appropriate for your organization. Consider the following advertisement from an executive search firm:

> *The XYZ organization is introducing an internal creative SWAT team called "Big Ideas." This team will be comprised of highly creative, entrepreneurial individuals who will be given a free rein to create and execute. They will be responsible for identifying*

new ideas, and selling those ideas within the business units of XYZ. This team will have limited supervision, but will have the complete support and backing of the President and Vice President of Marketing. Please send résumé and current salary to (executive search firm).

If you were employed by the XYZ organization, would you recommend this team structure? Is this the best approach to bringing diversity of thought to the XYZ organization? How would the creation of the "Big Ideas" team be viewed by other employees of the XYZ organization?

While this approach might work with certain organizations, the major challenge that this structure creates is the integration, both socially and technically, of this group's work with that of the mainstream organization. On a technical basis, how will this group know which ideas fit or do not fit the strategic needs of the business? Once these ideas are approved by top management, how will they be integrated with the business units so that they can be smoothly implemented? On a social basis, how will the other employees feel about this special team's "having the ear of top management" while they have to take the slower route for approvals? How will the other employees feel about the recruitment of this special team from "outside"? Will they feel that management believes that there were no qualified people currently within the XYZ organization? How does the creation of this team build the long-term innovation capacity of the XYZ organization?

Here are some alternative approaches that organizations have implemented with the objective of stimulating more innovation within their organizations:

- Some have designated a person to lead the innovation program and have granted titles, such as vice president of innovation, chief innovation officer, and director of innovation, to this new position. (While this approach signals to the organization that there is an innovation movement within, it might also put excessive responsibility on one person and have the unintended effect of marginalizing or diluting the organization's overall investment in innovation.)

- Another approach is to designate a team to lead innovation that is focused explicitly on developing new products or services. Lockheed and

Polaroid were the early adopters of the "skunkworks" method of focusing a special team on a specific challenge, away from the challenges of running the mainstream business. Kodak established an Office of Innovation, Molson Breweries established its Center of Innovation, and Procter & Gamble set up a special Corporate New Ventures Group to do just that. This approach is beneficial in that the team can focus on the specific challenge and develop ideas faster. If personnel are not available within the organization, skunkworks teams can be outsourced or staffed with a wide range of external personnel with specialized expertise. (The downside of the special-teams approach is the possible difficulty of integrating the ideas back into the mainstream of the organization. The idea might have been developed using a different business model than that which is available in the core business. Also, the receivers of the innovation, the core business, must approach the idea with the same attitude toward innovation, or else the spirit of the idea might fade as it makes its way through the system toward implementation.)

- The organization may choose to partner with an incubator organization whose role it is to create and develop new ideas. Once the idea is developed to a specific stage, it is spun-off to a newly created business unit or licensed or sold outright to another organization. (The downside to this approach is that it focuses the innovation effort solely on the research and development function for new products and limits the organization's view of the potential for innovation in all other areas of the organization. This fragments and isolates the organization's innovation efforts instead of aligning the organization behind the innovation agenda.)

- Another approach is to designate a team to lead the organization's innovation efforts by focusing not just in the new-products area but across many areas of the organization. Ideas can be identified for existing products and services, new products and services, new processes, and new business models. This team is the organization's "Navy Seals of Innovation." Some teams or departments might be natural early adopters and, as such, would be the best choice for leading the organization's innovative efforts. By showcasing this team's efforts and results, top management might be able to generate a positive response and thus pull innovation through the rest of the organization instead of having to push the innovation initiative on the organization. (The downside to this approach is twofold. First, elevating this team to special status might cause others within the organization to feel that the responsibility for innovation lies only with this special team and not with them—"You do innovative things and we'll do it the old way." Second, the activities of this team might not be integrated or aligned with the rest of the organization.)

- Yet another approach is to create innovation champions and teams who are integrated cross functionally throughout the organization. BP (British Petroleum) trained forty-eight Innovation Crusaders to spread the passion and skill for innovation management throughout its organization. 3M established GRITs (grass roots innovation teams) to support its objective of becoming the most innovative enterprise and to empower the creative potential of every individual at 3M. These teams understand the needs of the business and know how innovation-management techniques can be applied for the organization's benefit. Innovation champions and teams can infiltrate the organization with a common language and approach toward innovation.

The team structure that is chosen depends on the goals of the specific development project and the interest the organization has in creating its overall capacity for innovation. These various approaches highlight the need to view innovation from a systems thinking point of view. Consider the organization-wide implications of creating special positions and teams and the challenges associated with integrating innovations into the mainstream organization.

Ask yourself if the special positions or teams that you are about to create in your organization will encourage more widespread innovation or hinder it. Ask yourself what else you can do to create organizational-wide innovation.

Seek Greater Awareness of the Organization

In addition to gaining greater awareness of ourselves and our teams, we can benefit from gaining greater awareness of our organizations. An organization is simply a large team made up of many smaller teams who are connected by their pursuit of common goals. Organizational design is simply the *framework* that gives orderly structure to this large team.

Many organizations are now facing the fact that their organizational designs, including structure, climate, rewards, and training, are no longer addressing the growing complexity of the interrelationships between the teams of employees and their suppliers, partners, customers, and even competitors. Some teams still struggle to operate as separate entities despite the growing pressure to lower their boundaries and work more closely with others. The organization can no longer be viewed as a closed system. Instead, it needs to be viewed as an open, networked, and overlapping system where the right people can be connected with the right ideas in the fastest possible time. Ideas need to be moved quickly from team to team, and both approval and implementation of these ideas need to be performed at lightning speed.

Our traditional, hierarchical pyramid structures might not represent the best organizational design for the future. How much time do you waste trying to fit today's work into the existing processes of your antiquated structures? Is it time to evolve to a structure that would deliver faster response times and less duplication? Is it time to change your organizational structure to reflect the latest shift in technology, customer base, or availability of talent? Perhaps it is time to revisit your organizational structure to determine the optimal flow of information, work, and decision-making power for the future.

Is Your Organization in an Innovation Rut?

Innovation cannot thrive in organizations that are in an Innovation Rut! To help you determine whether your organization appears to be in an Innovation Rut, take a look at the twenty-five statements in Figure 7-1 and place a checkmark beside the statements that reflect the current state of affairs in your organization.

Consider your total score. As in golf, the lower the score, the better. If your score consisted of eight or fewer checkmarks, congratulations! Your organization seems to be on its way to becoming an Innovation Powerhouse. If your score consisted of nine to sixteen checkmarks, your organization could definitely benefit from implementing an innovation agenda. However, if your score consisted of more than seventeen checkmarks, your organization is undoubtedly in an Innovation Rut and needs to take corrective action immediately.

Figure 7-1. Innovation Rut checklist.

Agree (✓)	Statement
1 _____	Our products or services have lost their competitive edge.
2 _____	We lack consensus on what we would like to see happen within our organization in the next few years.
3 _____	We spend more time on discussing the present and the past than we do on looking to the future.
4 _____	We spend more time on internal issues than in pleasing our external customers.
5 _____	We rarely acknowledge and discuss our weaknesses.
6 _____	We rarely invite "outsiders" in to give us another perspective.
7 _____	We've stopped challenging the "way it's done around here."
8 _____	Valuable information is being held too tightly and not shared.
9 _____	Our planning process is inadequate for today's marketplace.
10 _____	We don't take the time to discuss alternative approaches or options for improvement.
11 _____	We think too small when we could be thinking BIG.
12 _____	We don't spend enough time identifying new ideas.
13 _____	We don't spend enough time developing new ideas.
14 _____	Great ideas often get blocked in our "system."
15 _____	Most of our ideas are incremental ideas or very small changes in what we are already doing.
16 _____	Our decision-making processes are too slow.
17 _____	I am unsure how decisions are made.
18 _____	Our organization is bureaucratic and has too many layers, rules, and policies.
19 _____	Good ideas are often underfunded.
20 _____	Good ideas are often understaffed.
21 _____	People complain that our organization is not very innovative.
22 _____	Innovation efforts are not rewarded or recognized.
23 _____	Good people are leaving our organization for better opportunities elsewhere.
24 _____	There is too much internal competition.
25 _____	People aren't really enjoying their work.

Total number of checks =

Top Ten Characteristics of Innovative Organizations

Based on my work with many leading organizations and applied research in the field of Innovation Management, I have concluded that innovative organizations have the following ten characteristics in common:

1. They encourage *all* employees, partners, and suppliers to take an active role in innovation.
2. They welcome new ideas and new approaches.
3. They look to the future to anticipate the customer's future needs.
4. They redefine the rules of the game and challenge complacent competitors.
5. They empower their customers with information and more control over the purchasing process.
6. They embrace new technology to strengthen their competitive advantage.
7. They employ internal processes that support innovation.
8. They allocate resources to find, develop, and implement new ideas.
9. They reward innovative efforts.
10. They move quickly.

How many of these top ten characteristics does your organization possess?

Innovation Systems Architecture

So how do you move out of your Innovation Rut and achieve the Top Ten Characteristics of Innovative Organizations? How do you move beyond simply stating that "innovation is one of our objectives" to making innovation a central part of all organizational activities? How do you ensure that the capacity for innovation is developed over time versus simply a passing topic at the annual meeting? How can you as a leader plant the seeds of innovation throughout the organization?

The simple answer is to gain greater awareness of the potential for innovation by taking a systematic view toward innovation. By looking at innovation from a systems-thinking point of view (seeing how all the parts of the whole are connected), you can help your organization begin the process of aligning and guiding itself to a higher level of innovation performance.

In support of this systematic view toward innovation, my colleague Alex Pattakos and I developed a model called "Innovation Systems Architecture®." Innovation, in our view, can be *systematically* managed by considering all the diverse elements that are required to create and sustain the environment for innovation. The word "architecture" was selected since the model also focuses and incorporates the various building blocks that are needed to build a strong foundation for organizational innovation.

By considering the various elements of this model, you can start to build the innovation engine that will enable innovation to permeate your organization. The model has been designed to be easily understood so that everyone can gain awareness of how innovation can be implemented in all areas of the organization, how innovation can be sustained on an ongoing basis, and how everyone can play a role in improving their own as well as the organization's capacity for innovation.

Based on our extensive field research and practice, we have identified eight key dimensions or *pillars* that define the architecture for building and sustaining innovation. All eight of these pillars play an important role in creating innovation systems architecture. The eight pillars of the Innovation Systems Architecture (ISA) model are shown in Figure 7-2.

The pillars have intentionally been defined to be generic in order to describe universal requirements; therefore, they are not product-, service-, or sector-specific. This is an important criterion since the innovation standards need to be flexible enough to adjust to a wide range of industries and organizational environments.

The details of each pillar and examples of how you can implement innovation initiatives in each area or pillar are explained in Chapter 10.

Figure 7-2. The Innovation Systems Architecture ® Model

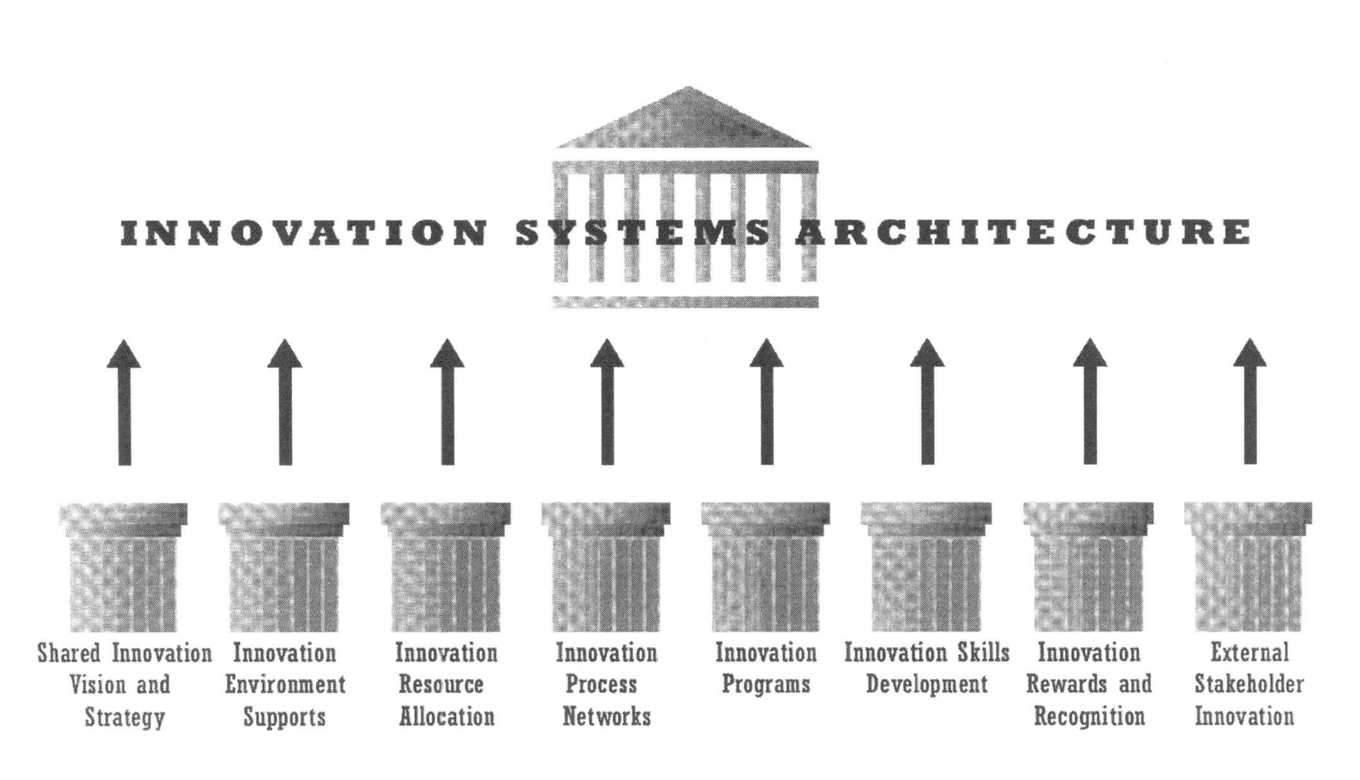

From *The Innovative Organization Assessment—A Holistic Approach*, by Alex Pattakos, Ph.D., and Elaine Dundon, MBA. © 2000 by Elaine Dundon, MBA. and Alex Pattakos, Ph.D. Reproduced with permission of Organization Design and Development Inc., King of Prussia, PA, USA.

CHAPTER 8

Ignite Passion

We all know about or are familiar with people who have lost their passion—those individuals who appear to have flat-lined or to be on cruise control throughout their lives. But we also know people who are extremely passionate about their work and their lives, who radiate positive energy and excitement wherever they go. It is not just the kind of work that these people are doing that is exciting; it is their attitude toward their work. Oprah Winfrey (talk-show host and philanthropist), Tiger Woods (world-class golfer), and Nelson Mandela (South African activist and former president) all put their hearts and souls into manifesting their human spirit and potential through their work. If we are open to it, their passion can be contagious.

Passion is also about linking creativity with a deeper purpose. Even when faced with tough situations, passionate people seem to find a deeper meaning to guide themselves. If you have a chance to visit Seattle's Pike Street Fish Market and witness first-hand the workers who were profiled in the book and video called *Fish!* you will see passion. Not only will you have a chance to watch these workers toss large fish back and forth among their team, you will also enjoy their wonderful and very entertaining sense of humor. If these individuals can bring passion to selling fish day in and day out, surely bringing more passion to your work and workplace should not be as challenging.[1]

What Is Passion?

So what do we mean by the word "passion"? *The Concise Oxford Dictionary* defines passion as "strong emotion or strong enthusiasm." To show your passion for something, therefore, requires you to display your enthusiasm from within. When you put your heart and soul into what you are doing, you are tapping into your strong emotional force or, in other words, your passionate self! The more you tap into this emotional force, the more you are filled with positive energy.

Why Have We Lost Our Passion?

Why have so many people lost their passion? Why, as Dee Hock asks in his book *Birth of the Chaordic Age*, are employees so alienated from their work?[2] While the answers may be many, here are my reasons why people may be losing passion:

1. ***Too much choice.*** The more choices a person has (in fact, the more freedom they have to make these choices), the more overwhelmed they may feel. They feel too much pressure to make too many choices in their jobs without having the necessary support from others.

2. ***Too many projects and not enough support.*** Many people lose passion when they feel unsure of their ability to complete their projects on time and in the manner that they feel is best warranted. Many organizations have eliminated positions through downsizing but are still employing the same processes or expecting the same results with a reduced resource base. Loss of passion is exacerbated when priorities are not reestablished in accordance with the weaker resource base or with a change in direction. When employees can't complete projects in the way they desire, they feel defeated.

3. ***Weak decision-making processes.*** Many employees complain either that they do not understand how decisions are made in their team and in their organization or that the decision-making processes are too slow.

4. ***Fear and anxiety.*** The uncertainty surrounding one's ability to hold on to a certain position within an organization can lead to increased fear and anxiety, which, in turn, can lead to decreased job performance and the loss of creativity. If someone fears the loss of their job, they will be less likely to take risks and may attempt to hide any potential signs of weakness to avoid becoming the next candidate for downsizing. If this fear is not addressed, they may lose the passion for embracing anything new and innovative.

5. ***Pursuit of extrinsic rewards.*** I will always remember the interview I conducted to fill a vacant marketing position on my team at Kraft General Foods. One of the candidates for the position was a woman who was working in another department at Kraft. When I asked her why she was interested in working with my marketing team, she replied, "The job pays better than my current job does." I was shocked. No mention of any passion for the actual job or for learning more about how to market a product to a target consumer group. No mention of any interest in wanting to work with a team of energetic, passionate marketers! How many more people are focusing so much on extrinsic rewards instead of pursuing a deeper attachment to the actual work?

6. ***Cynical humor.*** Although we may not be able to blame the lack of passion in our organizations on Scott Adams, the creator of the Dilbert comic strip, we do need to stay aware of the implications of such a cynical mindset. Unfortunately, Scott Adams is just reflecting the drama that occurs in many of our organizations, where employees and managers have lost their passion and have turned to cynical humor as a deflection for their serious lack of true meaning and passion in their work.

7. ***Stifled.*** Too often, people are encouraged to keep their passion under wraps. "It's not acceptable to show emotion when you work for the government." They soon stop bringing their true selves to work and, instead, dull their senses throughout the day. New employees, who are naturally full of innovative ideas, are encouraged to mimic "how things are done around here." Too often, passionless managers spread the virus by teaching others to stifle passion for innovative thinking.

8. ***No time.*** Many people say that there is no time to be passionate about looking for and developing new ideas. "I don't have time to think." "I don't have any time to innovate."

People may have lost their passion for these reasons. They may also have heard too many Passion Killers. For example:

> "Bob, give me an idea of how we could increase our inventory levels."
>
> "We could look into scheduling three shifts instead of two."
>
> "We thought of that already. Don't you have any practical ideas?"

So much of our training has been focused on building the skills to rip apart, marginalize, or criticize new ideas. While being able to see the merits and the weaknesses of an idea are indeed two skills that are needed for innovation, it is the balance of these two skills that is the issue. In most situations, the scales are tipped in favor of the weaknesses.

As Groucho Marx said, "Whatever it is, I'm against it." Here is a list of Passion Killers. How many have you heard in your organization? How many have you said?

Figure 8-1. Passion Killers.

We're not ready for that idea yet.

We're too busy.

It's too hard to implement.

If it's such a great idea, why hasn't anyone thought of it before?

It's all right in theory, but it would never work here.

If we let you do that, then everyone will want to do that.

It's a bad idea.

That's not your job.

It's too radical a change.

It's against company policy.

The president will never go for it.

Head Office will never go for it.

Let's give it some more thought.

We won't get the budget for it.

It's never been tried before.

We tried that before and it didn't work.

(Figure 8-1, continued) Passion Killers.

It's not a priority.
Let's put it on hold for now.
It's not a good time.
We've always done it this way.
Don't rock the boat.
Have you lost your mind?
We don't have the resources.
It won't work in this organization.
It wasn't invented here.
That breaks all the rules.
It will cost too much.
It's ahead of its time.
We're not ready for that.
It's too big for us to handle.
Let's wait.
That's a stupid idea.
It won't work.
Why would you want to do that?

What happens if we listen to all those criticisms? We end up back where we started. Hearing these Passion Killers—even the anticipation of hearing these Passion Killers—can stifle innovation. My two favorite Passion Killers are: "We haven't done that before" and "We've done that before!" It seems like these two Passion Killers are a Catch-22.

You have only so much energy. You can spend it being positive or you can spend it being negative. If you have 50,000 thoughts a day, what percentage of them are positive thoughts and what percentage of them are negative thoughts?

Ask yourself:

- Do you find it easier to criticize an idea than to support it? Why?
- How many of these Passion Killers do you find yourself saying each day?
- What is happening to all the good ideas in your organization?

Passion Supporters

Some seeds will fall on fertile soil, while others will fall on the pavement where they will find no nourishment and will be wasted. In order for innovation to flourish, new ideas must be supported. Surround yourself with passionate people who give your ideas the support they need. Support others' ideas and ask them to support yours. How many of these Idea Supporters are you using on a regular basis?

Figure 8-2. Passion Supporters.

Terrific	You're the best
You outdid yourself again	Go for it
Keep up the great work	Right on
Wonderful	That's top rate
Now you're cooking	Let's do it
Well done	I'm behind you
Wow	I wish I'd thought of that
I knew you could do it	That's a great idea
I'm glad you're on my team	I think it will work
That's your best work ever	That will really shake up the industry
You're right on target	The president will love this idea

Passion at the Individual Level

As individuals, we all want the opportunity to free our entrepreneurial spirit. Look what happened in Silicon Valley during the early dot-com days. Many individuals, including some hot teens, shook up the establishment with their passion and enthusiasm for finding and launching new business ideas. Most of them did it because they loved what they were doing. (Of course, a few pursued their ventures primarily as a means to fill their time and make money.) Wouldn't you like to be more like these passionate people who can't sleep because of the excitement of their work instead of like those who can't sleep because of the stress of their work?

Passion is the intensity we feel when we engage in an activity or project that deeply interests us. It is the life energy we receive and draw upon from doing what we love! In our chaotic world, it is important to know what makes or will make us more passionate about our work and about life in general. The more that you can align your personal values with your work, the more likely you are to find the deeper purpose in what you are doing, and the more passionate you will become.

Work should not just be about tasks and projects that need to be completed. Rather it should be a manifestation of our individuality and have a deeper sense of meaning in our lives. Whatever challenge you are facing, whatever your job responsibilities may be, it is always beneficial to try to rise up above the task or project and see both the bigger picture and the deeper meaning of what you are trying to achieve. Think of a night watchman, for example. By providing security for the team, he is helping others relax throughout the night. Think of an investigator for the U. S. Food and Drug Administration (FDA). She is committed to the higher purpose of ensuring that the prescription drugs many citizens use actually produce the intended results and, in doing so, she is guarding the public health. Take the time to identify the importance of your work and focus on it.

Stay focused on what you can contribute to yourself, your team, and your organization. Every organization needs inspired employees who will find and implement innovative ideas that will truly make a difference in their work. Are you fulfilling your potential?

In order to sustain your passion, you need to block out the cynics and focus on your purpose and contribution to the work of the organization. While you cannot always change the situation in which you find yourself, you can always change your reaction to it. Dr. Viktor Frankl, psychiatrist, existential philosopher, and author of the now-classic book *Man's Search for Meaning*, taught us about transcending even the most catastrophic situations. Having survived the horrors of the Nazi concentration camps, including several years at Auschwitz, Dr. Frankl underscored the importance of what he found to be the basic intrinsic motivation of all human beings—the search for meaning. Even in situations of despair and suffering, he observed that people can find meaning if they exercise their ultimate freedom to choose their attitude toward the situation. Passion in this sense is as much a state of mind as it is the behavioral manifestation of enthusiasm for something. By learning how to *detach* oneself from a given situation, and then *transcend* it in favor of the bigger picture, it is possible, according to Dr. Frankl, to maintain the flame of passion throughout one's life. Dr. Frankl suggested that "It's not what happens to you that is important, it's how you choose to respond that matters."[3]

Focus on what is right about the situation instead of what is wrong, and seek to learn from it. Cutbacks, layoffs, and downsizing are affecting every sector in every industry in every country. Realize this and move on. Instead of letting circumstances bring you down, instead of walking into work each morning barely alive, walk in with passion and say, "I'm glad to be here. Let's make something great happen!" Put the passionate spirit back into your work and into the lives of all you meet. If you are not passionate about your work, how do you expect others around you to be? As Ghandi said, “You must be the change you want in the world.”

Set aside time in your day to think about the BIG Picture and how you can find new ideas to help your team and organization. Some companies, like 3M, encourage their employees to set aside 15 percent of their time to explore new ideas and projects. Other organizations have implemented “No-Meeting Fridays” to give their employees more thinking time, including the opportunity and freedom to reflect and challenge themselves in new ways. Others have decreased the number of internal reports and presentations required so that employees can have more time and flexibility to work on “value-added” initiatives. And other organizations rely on structured time-management systems to ensure that employees take the time to innovate.

Ask yourself:

- Are you engaged in activities that deeply interest you?
- Are you fulfilling your potential?
- Are you blocking out cynics and other negative influences?
- Are you being the change you want to see in the world?
- Are you giving yourself enough time to be innovative?

Passion at the Team Level

It is important to understand the difference between the stated culture and the real culture. Many teams post a list of the principles and practices that comprise their stated culture on their boardroom wall but then do nothing to correct behavior that deviates from this stated culture. Real culture relies more on the personalities and behaviors of the team members than on a list of desired attributes.

There are at least four key Passion Drivers at work:

- Doing challenging work
- Having a sense of ownership in the ability to identify and implement one’s innovative ideas

- Being recognized and rewarded for one's innovative work
- Having the opportunity to work with other passionate people in a passionate environment

Wouldn't it be wonderful if everyone could recapture the passion that the founders of their organization once had? Wouldn't it be great, for example, if Kraft Foods could replicate the passion J. L. Kraft had in the early days or if Hewlett-Packard could replicate the passion Bill Hewlett and David Packard generated when they began working in the now-famous garage in Palo Alto? Wouldn't it be great if all employees of the Dell Computer Corporation could feel the rush of excitement that came from receiving the company's first order?

The employees at Walt Disney World, or cast members, as they are often called, share their passion to create a wonderful experience for their customers or guests.[4] When you visit the Disney theme parks, you can tell that their employees are excited about what they do and what their organization does for the entertainment world. The founders and employees of the Powerbar organization also share a common passion for their work. Powerbar is an energy bar that was created for athletes by athletes. Most of the employees of Powerbar are sports enthusiasts, so they find it easy to transfer their passion for sports to the manufacturing and marketing of their top-selling energy bar. Tom's of Maine, Ben & Jerry's, and Southwest Airlines are examples of other organizations that believe in employees' bringing their personal passion to work.

The employees at Southwest Airlines are encouraged to be creative and make improvements on their own initiative. Co-founder Herb Kelleher knew that, in order to truly create an environment for innovation, he had to be willing to grant his employees the freedom to make decisions "on the spot," decisions that they felt were in the best interest of the organization. By pushing decision-making down to the levels where it was most productive, he signaled to the organization that Southwest Airlines truly values it employees. Employees' passion for their jobs rubs off on the customers. If you fly with Southwest Airlines, you can see and feel the passion in the air![5]

Many people feel more passion when they feel a sense of ownership in an idea. If a person is granted the opportunity to continue to work on an idea once it has been approved, they will feel a stronger sense of ownership and pride in seeing the idea realize the potential they had originally promised.

It is important to recognize the originators of ideas as well as those who implemented them. It is often the case that a person who joined the team in the eleventh hour, as a new idea was being launched into the marketplace, received all the glory while the development team, who spent the previous year shaping and reshaping the idea, receives little or no recognition. How does your organization recognize innovators and their contributions?

While some organizations are good at recognizing the champions behind the innovations they actually implemented, other organizations, such as Radical Entertainment, a video-game development company located in Vancouver, Canada, go a little bit farther. If Radical Entertainment decides, for one reason or another, that it is not going to pursue the development of an employee's idea, that employee is welcome to show his new video game idea to other organizations. How's that for recognizing employees' need for inspiration and sense of ownership?[6]

Ask your team:

- Do we have a passion for pleasing our customers?
- Do we feel free to make decisions?
- Do we feel a sense of ownership for our ideas?
- Do we formally recognize our team members' ideas?
- Do we all know each other or are we just viewing each other as people completing projects and tasks?

A Passionate Physical Environment

Imagine two reception areas: The first exudes excitement. The sun shines brightly through the many skylights and rests gently on the marble floor. On one wall is a vivid display of the company's product line while on the other wall is a display of letters from satisfied customers. On the coffee table are copies of the company's latest promotional materials and a jar of jellybeans that just happen to match the corporate colors. The receptionist smiles kindly and asks if the directions to the building were easy to follow.

The other reception area screams depression. Three tattered old office chairs surround one old coffee table. The remains of this morning's newspaper (the business section is missing) lie beside two copies of *Newsweek* dated a few months ago. A lonely plant leaning slightly to the right stands limply beside the reception counter. On the reception counter is a small sign: Please ring bell.

Which environment shouts, "We're excited you're here. We want to work with you"? Which environment communicates the company's passion? Which company seems more innovative? With which company would you rather work?

Passionate environments truly vibrate at a higher level. You can just feel the energy when you walk into the building. While there may not be conclusive studies to prove that there is a relationship between the physical environment and increased profitability, both intuition and anecdotal evidence suggest that there may be. First, one of the factors influencing new employees' choice of employer is the environment in which they will be spending the majority of their waking hours. Sccond, space is a symbol of the excitement and pride that employees have for the business. If employees have the opportunity to work in an environment that supports this excitement and pride, they will potentially be more passionate about their work, which could lead to higher productivity. Third, if employees have the opportunity to work in a passionate environment that also celebrates their individuality, they might feel more open to sharing their "crazy, innovative" ideas instead of feeling pressure to conform to the "way its always been around here." (Of course, other factors such as innovation-process networks and cultural and financial support for new ideas also play a key role in determining the level of innovation produced by a team or organization.)

The advertising agency GSD&M believes that there is a relationship between physical environment, an energetic culture, and creative output. Their building in Texas is designed to stimulate interaction among employees and therefore has more than fifty rooms of various sizes where coworkers can meet and share ideas.

Some organizations are investigating or have built separate "creativity centers" within their existing office spaces. These centers typically represent a cross between a resource center with access to magazines, videos, and other materials, and a community center, with comfortable chairs, strobe lights, toys, squirt guns, and even karaoke machines! However, some organizations, like Lucent Technologies with its Ideaverse concept, have disbanded their creativity centers for a variety of reasons. In some instances, organizations have found that the centers were difficult to maintain once they were established or that workers were not using the center for the intended purpose.

A better and clearly more comprehensive approach is to incorporate passion and innovation into the design throughout the building. Begin with an inviting lobby that signals innovation. Then you might want to add a Hall of Fame to profile your top innovators. Think about your own offices and conference rooms—not all offices and conference rooms need to look the same. Add excitement through different aesthetic treatments. Create innovative names for your conference rooms. At TELUS Mobility, for example, training rooms were named Insight, Imagination, Mind Bender, Brain Waves, Mental Muscle, Intuition, and Perception. Likewise, their lunchrooms and lounge were named Reflection and Planet Balance. The Planet Balance room is decorated with comfortable chairs, a junk box, a free espresso bar, and a "chill-out" area complete with a star-gazing ceiling.[7]

Make room for "Innovation Expos" where exciting projects can be displayed. Add whiteboards and writing surfaces in places such as hallways, stairwells, and lunchrooms where people meet. Add a variety of stimuli—perhaps examples from your customers or clients—to your conference rooms. Many companies, such as Rubbermaid, have a stimuli room where they collect examples of their competitors' products for analysis and discussion. They also have a room where they display their latest and greatest products.[8] Consider contacting companies like Steelcase, Herman Miller, Keilhauer, and One Workplace that specialize in helping other organizations design the optimal working environments for their employees. You might also want to consider the allocation of some quiet spaces where employees can relax and recharge their passion batteries. There is an increasing interest in the design of creative workspaces, including the application of feng shui principles.

For some people, of course, creating an innovative environment within their workplace is not a priority. In these cases, create a special environment for innovative thinking by just encouraging employees to use a *different* environment. Entering a new environment—taking a walk in the woods, going for a drive in the car, or sitting alone in a basement workshop—can provide the kind of innovative environment people need to relax and tap into their creative spirit.

Until now, many leaders did not consider their environment to be an important element in stimulating passion and innovative thinking. Ask yourself the following questions:

- Is our environment inviting?
- Does our environment communicate who we are, what we do, and what we are most proud of?
- Do we use color, lighting, art, greenery, sound, and other aesthetically pleasing techniques to convey excitement and energy?
- Do we have a good mixture of group meeting spaces to fit the needs of our team to meet formally or informally?
- Does our environment change or evolve as our work evolves?
- Does our environment communicate that we are an innovative organization?

Remember though, designing a passionate physical space does not guarantee that the team will magically become more innovative! You must also consider the psychological environments (climate, rewards, and recognition) as well as the processes, resources, and skills development that are needed to support innovation within your organization.

CHAPTER 9

Take Action

"Five frogs are sitting on a log. Four decide to jump off. How many are left?"[1] You might think this is a simple riddle. "Why, one frog, of course," you respond, thinking "That was an easy and straightforward question." It's not until someone else in the crowd answers "five frogs" that you stop and examine the riddle again. You see, even though four frogs *decided* to jump off, there is nothing in the riddle to indicate that they actually jumped. One of the lessons provided by this simple riddle is that there is a big difference between deciding to do something and actually doing it! Indeed, the Nike slogan "Just Do It" is often much easier said than done. However, innovation, by definition, requires that a creative idea be implemented or acted upon in order to add value.

Simply put, great ideas are not "innovative" unless they are successfully implemented. The critical factor is not the number of ideas that you or your team may have, but the successful implementation of the ideas. There are many examples of organizations that were on the right track but failed to take action, took too little action, or moved too slowly with their ideas.

Digital Research had access to the technology of the revolutionary 16-bit operating system (DOS) but failed to capitalize on this idea, thereby leaving the door open for Bill Gates to network with IBM and lay the groundwork for what would become the Microsoft Corporation. Atari, Commodore, and Kaypro are other examples of organizations that were once "king of the hill" or industry leaders but failed to understand the need for a sense of urgency when it came to finding and implementing new ideas.

Many people have been conditioned to believe that once a certain level of "success" has been achieved, they can sit back and reap the benefits—"Once I get my MBA degree . . . ," "Once our business has the largest share of the market . . ." "Once our government agency wins an award for performance excellence . . ." If only that were the case! Although we should, of course, celebrate and enjoy our successes, we should also always be aware that the world is constantly evolving and that we therefore need to be constantly *innovating*. In today's world, there is no such thing as a "sustainable competitive advantage." Every organization is vulnerable to competition, even those at the top of their field or industry. Take, for example, McDonald's restaurants, generally recognized as leading the way into fast-food heaven. Now McDonald's needs to *innovate* in order to deal with the very serious threat of mad cow disease and the dire impact that perceptions about this disease could have on its hamburger business. Another example is Bausch & Lomb, well known for leading the way with contact lens solutions. Now Bausch & Lomb needs to *innovate* in order to deal with the trend toward disposable lenses and laser eye surgery.

As Stephen Covey so wisely said in his groundbreaking book *The 7 Habits of Highly Effective People*, Habit #1 is Be Proactive.[2] So many great organizations and the people aligned with them fail to reach their full potential due to lack of action. We all know that words on a page by themselves will not transform an organization. Action will.

The Third Stage of the Nine-Step Innovation Process: Action

The final stage of the Nine-Step Innovation Process involves building the strategic ideas into full business concepts and plans. These plans are reviewed in accordance with the strategic Innovation Goalposts, which were discussed in Chapter 4, making acceptance more realistic and more plausible. From here, the ideas are implemented and reviewed for shared learning. The specific steps in the *Action* stage are (1) developing the Innovation Roadmap, (2) gaining commitment, and (3) implementing the Innovation Roadmap. Let's take a look at each of these three steps.

Developing the Innovation Roadmap

Categorize your business ideas or concepts into different groups, such as: (a) ideas on hold—relevant but not applicable for the next few years; (b) ideas to investigate further before a decision can be made; (c) fast-track ideas for presentation, development, and implementation; and (d) fast-track, high-potential ideas for immediate presentation, development, and implementation.

You may want to apply different criteria to different types of projects. For example, projects that represent products or services to be introduced to the marketplace in the next two years might be subject to different criteria than projects or services that will be introduced later.

In order to build these concepts into full business plans, revisit the six BIG-Picture criteria. These criteria will help you develop a strategic idea into a full business concept and will also help you prepare your idea for presentation.

1. ***The big idea must be simple.*** What is your BIG idea? Good ideas should be simple and easy to explain. A weak seed cannot grow into a healthy plant, no matter how rich the soil! If an idea starts out as a weak idea, everyone will have to spend extra time to fix it along the way.

2. ***The idea must support the overall business strategy.*** How does this idea fit with the Innovation Goalposts discussed at the beginning of the project? How does this idea support the overall strategic vision and path the organization has chosen to pursue? How does this idea fit with the organization's other products, services, and programs? How does this idea fit with the organization's core competencies?

3. ***The idea must be "distinctly new and better."*** What problem are you seeking to solve or eliminate? Why do we need this idea? Why do current or future customers need this idea? What new value does this idea bring? How will this idea change the organization or the marketplace?

4. ***The idea must be proven.*** Even if you feel your idea is new to the marketplace, find examples of other ideas that are relatively similar to your idea and share those with your team. Most people want to minimize risk. Unfortunately, people tend not to believe in the potential of new ideas unless someone else, especially someone whom they admire, has already done it. Every manager wants to balance the risks associated with new ideas. How can you link your idea with another idea that others already know or have had experience with? Have other organizations succeeded with a similar idea or with parts of your idea? Finding examples of how similar ideas or idea attributes have generated positive results for other organizations will lower the perception of risk for your new idea. Also summarize any market research results you have on the idea.

5. ***The idea must be profitable.*** Show them the money! What will be the revenue gained from your idea, and how high can the revenue go? Show how the idea can be expanded to attract even more revenue in the future. Demonstrate how the idea will deliver social benefits. What kinds of investments are needed to support the idea? Will it deliver good value for the funding required? Determine how the idea will be funded.

6. ***The idea must be quickly and easily implemented.*** Determine how easy the implementation will be by highlighting the steps involved, the timing, the resource needs, and the implementation team. List the changes that will be needed in order to implement this new idea in terms of team members' roles, core competencies, and any necessary process changes.

In addition to these six BIG-Picture criteria, please refer to Appendix E for a more extensive list of criteria that you and your team might want to use to turn your strategic idea into a full business concept. Writing down your answers to these criteria questions will result in clearer and more disciplined thinking.

Writing the Innovation Roadmap

Once you have thought through your new business concept, you may wish to prepare a written Innovation Roadmap. Instead of preparing a thirty-page plan or a five-inch thick stack of PowerPoint slides, why not write a simple yet focused six-page Innovation Roadmap? Here is a template that can be used for all Innovation Roadmaps—at the corporate, business-unit, category, and specific product, service, or program level. The six-page Innovation Roadmap template includes:

Page 1: Learning (key lessons learned from your review of the current state of your business, your customers, your competition, and other elements of the marketplace)

Page 2: Future (your predictions for the future re: customers, the marketplace, competition, technology, and other challenges)

Page 3: Vision (your vision or future destination, the direction or path to reach this vision, and your BIG idea)

Page 4: Requirements (core competencies and resources needed to achieve the vision, path, and BIG idea)

Page 5: Action Plans (a summary of key action plans with timing and responsibility)

Page 6: Financials (financial resources and forecasts)

Challenge yourself to include only key pieces of information. Use bullets or point form and charts to summarize the information.

Gaining Commitment

We have all had experiences where our ideas have been rejected by managers who obviously lacked vision or "just didn't get it." Looking back on some of these experiences, we may come to realize that perhaps we could have done a few things differently in order to package our ideas so others could see the light. There might have been things we could have done to reduce the amount of uncertainty surrounding our new idea. Spending the time to prepare and package ideas is, therefore, a critical step in the innovation process, especially for creative people who are facing the challenge of having to prove the merits of their new ideas to a very linear, logic-based audience.

Understanding Your Audience

An important step in preparing and packaging your idea is to focus on who is "buying" it. Who is the appropriate audience for your idea? Is this audience ready to discuss a new idea?

Not everyone is the same, and not everyone will focus on the same aspects of your idea. In my experience, there are four types of people in the world: those who want to see the numbers, those who want to focus on tasks, those who want to focus on people, and those who want to focus on BIG-Picture strategy. Take time to determine who is in your audience. What type of ideas do they usually support? What type of questions do they usually ask? Do they want to know the numbers? Do they want to know the details of the tasks needed to implement the plan? Do they want to know the impact the plan will have on the people in the organization or on the customer? Do they want to know how the plan fits with the organization's overall strategy?

It is rare that an idea is accepted at its initial presentation. Recognize that your audience may be at different stages of the innovation-decision process.[3] Each buyer, whether they are buying an idea or a product, goes through several stages before taking action. These stages include knowledge, persuasion, decision, implementation, and confirmation. It is therefore prudent to gauge what stage your audience is at in the buying cycle and to be realistic about how quickly you can move them to making a decision!

Preparing a Prototype

Many ideas are rejected because they are misunderstood. In this regard, you may want to consider developing a prototype of your idea so that others can gain a better understanding of its various elements. A prototype is simply an illustration or sample that represents the essence of your idea in its preliminary stages of development. The design firm IDEO is famous for developing numerous prototypes and doing so very rapidly. You can use a prototype to make your idea come alive for your audience.

Prototyping at IDEO is part of its iterative creation process so that both team members and clients can make their mistakes and discoveries as soon as possible. "Quick prototyping is about acting before you've got the answers, about taking chances, stumbling a little, but then making it right."[4] By asking for and getting early feedback from the analysis of the prototype, the design teams are able to gain a better understanding of the direction the project should take and are able to make rapid progress toward the completion of the project. As veteran IDEO studio head Dennis Boyle often says, "Never go to a meeting without a prototype."[5] If your idea is difficult to prototype or if a prototype of your idea is not available, find another object or several objects that illustrate your idea. This helps the audience visualize the potential.

Michael Schrage also espoused the virtues of rapid prototyping in his book *Serious Play*.[6] By offering several variations on the same idea theme and by providing a visual illustration of these idea options and their corresponding benefits, you can accelerate the presentation and understanding process.

Presenting Your Idea or Innovation Roadmap

Often people get so lost in the details of their idea or Innovation Roadmap that their audience loses its focus on the Simple Big Idea. Here is my simple Six-Step Selling Process that you can use to present your ideas. The process will help focus your audience, and yourself, on the important aspects of your idea. Your entire team may wish to follow the same Six-Step Selling Process when presenting their ideas so that it becomes second nature.

Figure 9-1. Six-Step Selling Process.

Step	Topic	Explanation
1	Groundwork	Describe the situation. Highlight the problem. Explain the implications if the problem intensifies or if the problem is not addressed immediately. Set the stage for the introduction of your simple big idea.
2	The Simple Big Idea	Present the simple big idea.
3	Brief Explanation	Give a brief explanation of how the simple big idea works.

Step	Topic	Explanation
4	The Benefits	Explain the benefits of adopting your simple big idea. Reference the Six BIG-Picture criteria: (1) Simple big idea, (2) supports the overall business strategy, (3) is distinctly new and better, (4) is proven, (5) is profitable, and (6) can be quickly and easily implemented.
5	Implementation Plan	Give the major highlights of your implementation plan.
6	Asking for Action	Ask the decision-maker for a decision. Tell them what you want them to do now that they have heard your presentation.

Go into the presentation with the assumption that your audience might not understand your new idea and that you therefore need to simplify your communications and walk them through your thought process step-by-step. If your idea is too difficult to understand, you already have a barrier between you as the seller and your audience as the buyer.

Keep your presentations simple and only offer facts or examples that support your big idea. Do not overload your audience with unnecessary details. Give them surface details and if they have specific questions, this is the time to "drill down" to give them more detailed explanations. Limit your use of jargon so that the audience can concentrate on your message, not get sidetracked by having to figure out what a word or concept means.

Create the demand for your idea as a solution to the problem or situation. When presenting, spend at least 25 percent of your time selling the problem and all its implications. The members of the audience must understand the context in which they are being asked to make a decision. Many times your audience might not have been privy to the information that you have regarding the severity or scope of the problem, or they might not understand the implications of ignoring the problem until it is too late. Realize that not everyone has your insight. Take the time to educate them on the extent of the problem. Try to gain a common understanding of the problem before you move into presenting your solution.

More than likely, your audience will support you if they believe in the power of the idea—that there is indeed a real problem and that you have a good solution for that problem. Your audience must believe your solution will work and will add value. People will fight you if they do not believe in the severity of the problem, if they don't think your idea will work, or if you present the idea in such a way as to totally confuse and irritate them.

Many presentations of valid ideas crumble into oblivion because the presenter uses too much jargon, gets lost in the details or, in general, is so out of touch with the audience's needs that the presentation falls on deaf ears.

Do you remember the passion and enthusiasm that you demonstrated when sharing your favorite object with others in grade school? Tap into that excitement. It is still in you! Sell your idea, don't just present it. Sell the dream of your idea, not simply all the details. Show how your idea will make a difference. Show your own passion and commitment if you want your audience to also have passion for your idea. As a presenter, it is important that you believe in your idea despite any opposition that you might face. As Gary Hamel suggests in *Leading the Revolution*, if they say, "Someone already tried this, and it didn't work," you say, "They didn't try it this way!"[7] Overall, the time and attention your audience will give you and your idea are directly proportionate to your level of passion.

The process of selling new ideas involves finding common ground—and points of resonance—between the presenter and the audience. Many people just start selling their ideas and leave little room for understanding how the audience might be viewing and receiving the presentation and, importantly, the potential of the innovative idea. It is important in this connection to engage the audience in authentic dialogue rather then simply talking *at* them. Connect with them on a much deeper level. Build a shared understanding of your proposal. Increase the chances of selling your new ideas. The best ideas are co-created by the seller and the buyer, so let the buyer have input into reshaping the idea.

Receiving an Idea

Just as the presenter has the responsibility to offer well-thought-out ideas, the audience has the responsibility to receive new ideas in an encouraging and motivating way. Besides reviewing the idea to determine whether it fits with the decision-making criteria, consider the larger implications of your comments as a receiver of the new idea.

- If you are rejecting the idea, are you doing so because you are resisting change? Why are you *really* stopping this idea?

- Are you unwilling to change what has made you successful in the past? Are you asking for too much rigorous evaluation, or are you setting the hurdles so high that very few ideas can ever make it through your review? Is the report or committee work you are asking for really necessary? By asking for more details or more committee work, are you giving the presenter the sign that the idea is really being put out to pasture? Will your evaluation process result in the approval of only ideas that mirror the existing work of the organization, or will you approve ideas that stretch the definition of the existing organization?

- Are you hiding behind complicated rules, policies, or bureaucracy so you do not have to risk making a decision? Are you evading your decision-making responsibility by using Passion Killers such as "the board or president will never go for this idea"?

- How are your comments affecting the presenter? Are you balancing your negative comments with positive ones? Are you motivating or inspiring the presenter to continue the search for new ideas?

- How can you link the presenter with others who can help develop the idea?

- Are you creating a sense of urgency for innovation?

If managers won't let good ideas through, the organization suffers from an obvious lack of progress in advancing its innovation objective.

It's a two-way street. Every organization needs a dual strategy for both presenting ideas and accepting new ideas. Many organizations, such as Singapore Airlines, are starting to offer training in how to accept as well as present ideas.

Overcoming Resistance to Your Idea or Innovation Roadmap

You may hear objections such as the Passion Killers discussed in Chapter 8. "We don't have any time." "We don't have any money." "It's too risky." "It will ruin our image." "We won't get the board's approval." Recognize that it is a hundred times easier for a person to say "no" than to say "yes." And the bigger the change required, the bigger the roadblocks in its path. If people do not have to change, or if they are not aware of the need for change, they will usually not make the effort.

Be aware that most people focus on what they have to give up with the current method rather than what they might gain from adopting the new idea. Understand how attached your audience is to the current approach or idea. Obviously, if people are happy with the current approach, a change in approach may not be viewed as necessary. Use discussion to get your audience to agree that the current approach is not optimal. A fundamental law of change is that if you want people to try something new and different, they have to be dissatisfied in some way with the current choice.

Kurt Lewin identified three different avenues to facilitate the process of unfreezing in order to encourage people to change. These avenues are:

1. ***Invalidation.*** Show that the current ways of doing things are no longer working. You will have to create tension and dissatisfaction with the status quo in order to get your audience to change.

2. ***Creation of guilt or anxiety.*** Forecast tough times ahead due to increased competition. Give examples of what might happen if the idea is not accepted. Highlight that everyone must be looking for new ideas.

3. ***Creation of psychological safety.*** Provide opportunities for training and practice, as well as support and encouragement, to overcome fears.

These avenues can, of course, be tried alone or in combination.[8]

The resistance to change might not be due to poor timing, limited resources, or a poor idea. It might be the result of lack of understanding of how the idea will be implemented. Recognize that even if the audience has bought into the problem definition and preferred solution you are offering, you must also offer them an easy implementation plan.

You also need to recognize that resistance to change does not emanate only from your audience. It can come from other departments, distribution partners, customers, or other stakeholders. They might not want to shake up the system with your new idea. Remember, people only embrace change if they think it is in their best interest to do so. How are you going to convince these groups that your new idea is worth the investment? Great innovators spend time figuring out how to get around the barriers of limited resources, company policies, and other peoples' resistance to change. You must be willing to readjust the Innovation

Roadmap to incorporate other peoples' concerns. Like the quarterback who tries different plays to advance the ball down the field, recognize that more than one play may be needed to advance your plan.

You might be able to overcome resistance to change by offering the opportunity for a trial implementation in order to help everyone manage the risk of accepting a new idea. By offering a trial, you will be able to show some progress toward your goal. As your managers start to see the benefits of your idea materialize, more support may be forthcoming. This concept is similar to the promotional tactic used by many marketers. In other words, provide a sample of your product. If the consumer likes your sample, he might buy the larger size. In essence, you are recommending base hits instead of expecting a home run right away.

Implementing the Innovation Roadmap

The last step in the Nine-Step Innovation Process is implementing the Innovation Roadmap. Release your roadmap or plan into action. Remember to apply enough pressure until the plan is implemented to ensure that people do not slip back into their old way of doing things or find other priorities to work on. Even though someone might have said they were committed to your plan, they may still be unsure about certain elements of the plan. Take the time to ensure that when someone says they are committed, this phrase means the same to you as it does to them. Keep an eye out for any roadblocks. There are always some. Implement and have your team follow a good project-management process that clearly outlines who will be involved at what stage, the tasks involved, and the expected completion dates of each of the tasks. As discussed in Chapter 6, find ways to expedite the implementation of your idea through parallel processing or by shortening the lead times for each task.

Make sure you and your team have reviewed the number of projects on your plate so that you can match the number of projects with the team's ability to develop and implement them. Is there really room for one more project? More projects do not always mean more results. Often more activity is counterproductive since the organizational resources are not being focused in the most productive manner. After all, three projects with great results are better than five projects with mediocre results. Perhaps the discussion of your new idea can spark a strategic discussion of where your own and your team's energies should be directed for the good of the overall organization. Perhaps your team can eliminate one or two other less valuable projects in order to have the time to focus on your new, more valuable project.

Adjust the implementation plan where needed and remember to review the experience so that learning—what worked, what didn't work, what should we do differently in the future—can be shared with all team members.

Implementation in the Marketplace

The strategies for selling a new idea in the marketplace are similar to those previously discussed for selling an idea internally within an organization. In order to persuade customers to change, they must be convinced that their current approach is not optimal and that switching to the new idea will be easy and profitable. For example, take the recent flood of television advertisements for long-distance telephone services. So many of the ads focused on the price of the service, comparing one company's five-cent plans to others' ten-cent plans. What was missing in these ads was the switching plan to make it easy for the customer: How do I switch from what I am using now to this new service? Do I need to change my phone number? How does it work with my local phone company? The focus of the communication should have been on the simple switching plan versus the small cost difference between telephone rates. In my opinion, this was the problem that needed to be solved for the customer, who already understood that alternative, lower-priced telephone services were available. The lack of information on how to switch may have prevented many consumers from buying the cheaper service.

Another example is Procter & Gamble's Dryel product. The concept behind this product is to encourage consumers to forgo the dry cleaners and simply use their clothes dryers instead. All they have to do is place their clothes in a Dryel bag with a Dryel sheet and then place this bag in the dryer. The big challenge facing Procter & Gamble is how to convince consumers to switch to this product when they have been conditioned all their lives not to put certain clothes in the dryer. Perhaps this idea just goes against the grain as did a previous similar product called Sweater Fresh.[9]

Do you have a solid plan to convince your customers to switch to your new idea?

Passion, Patience, and Perseverance

"Today's mighty oak is just yesterday's nut that held its ground." —ANONYMOUS

Remember, if you want others to believe in your idea, you need to be passionate about it yourself. Innovation is about challenging the status quo to find a distinctly new and better way. It is about the courage to stand alone for a while until others catch up. For this you need passion and patience! How did Alexander Graham Bell feel when he invented the telephone and people criticized his idea? People in his day thought he was crazy when he explained the ability to hear voices through a wire. If only his doubters could see the world today: How the telephone has progressed from the rotary dial phone to call waiting, call forwarding, call blocking, voice mail, conference calls, and e-mail!

Timing Is Important

Is your industry ready for your new idea? Take solace from the fact that many others who have gone before you have faced challenges in having their great ideas rejected. The inventors of battery-operated cars and electric cars are still waiting for the automobile and oil industry to accept alternative methods of transportation. Purveyors of homeopathic and naturopathic medicine are challenging the medical and pharmaceutical industries to accept alternative forms of health care. The Spice Girls and the Beatles, two famous pop music groups, were turned down many times before they found success.

Are consumers ready for your new idea? Will they resist switching from their current solutions? It took Kellogg's over a decade to convince consumers to switch from eating hot cereal to eating cold cereal. It took a long time for the Internet to make it into the mainstream. It was used by the military and by universities long before consumer-friendly Web browsers and programs made it more attractive to the general public.

Find Supporters

Find supporters who can help your cause. The key supporter for your idea might be your immediate supervisor, someone in another department, or someone on the executive team. At the early stages of idea development, go to where the energy behind the idea seems to be focused so that your idea receives the support it needs. Build a team of supporters who will help to *push* your idea through the various organization systems. Also try to identify the group of supporters who will *pull* your idea through the system. Who, in other words, will be helpful for advancing your cause? Gifford Pinchot, in his groundbreaking book *Intrapreneuring*, offered ten commandments of the "intrapreneur." Intrapreneurship refers to efforts by organizations to identify and support individuals or teams of individuals who wish to pursue an entrepreneurial idea for a new product or service. It also includes the adoption of managerial and organizational techniques that establish an environment in the organization that actively promotes *creative* behavior by its employees.[10] Three of his commandments for intrapreneurs are:

- Find people to help you.
- Work underground as long as you can.
- Honor your sponsors.

Also consider garnering support from the outside. Take, for example, the Hush Puppies rejuvenation. The classic American brushed-suede shoe had been in decline for some time. Then, in 1995, Hush Puppies quietly became hip in the clubs and bars in New York City, and designers began requesting the shoes for their fashion shows. Hush Puppies started showing up in advertisements, and soon the shoes became very popular with the youth of America. The influencers in this case were young people in the clubs in downtown New York City and a few fashion designers.[11]

Malcolm Gladwell, in his book *The Tipping Point*, calls this the Law of the Few.[12] Only a few key people are needed to support your idea. By identifying those people who are good connectors (those who know a lot of people and can connect you with the right people to help your cause), as well as by linking up with people who are great salespeople (those who can educate others about your cause), the job of selling your idea will become easier.

Repeat the Presentation of Your Idea

It is our natural tendency to forget some or all of what we have just heard as we move on to new tasks. As Professor Hermann Ebbinghaus discovered with the Law of the Forgetting Curve, human beings tend to forget quickly and to require information to be repeated in bits in order to alter this "curve."[13] Advertisers address this curve by showing their advertisements frequently in hopes that the message will register with consumers. Recognize that you may need to repeat your message on different occasions before you can gain commitment.

Repackage Your Idea

You may also wish to find more than one audience for your idea, or you may wish to find more than one application for the idea if the selling process is not going as smoothly as you would like. As with football, the direct route to the goal line is not always possible. You might have to try a different way to go around your opposition. You might need to make several small attempts instead of trying to score with one play. Sometimes what is needed is to take the spirit of your idea and repackage it in a different way so that the probability of acceptance is higher. When General Mills first introduced the Betty Crocker cake-mix product, consumers resisted using the cake mix because they felt that they should still be baking the old-fashioned way and that they were cheating if they used the cake mix! General Mills thought through this problem for a while and then came up with a brilliant idea: Why not reinvent the cake-mix product so that a consumer needed to add an egg? This way the consumers would feel as if they were actually baking. The revamped product soon gained great acceptance.

CHAPTER 10

Organizational Innovation

The preceding chapters introduced the seeds of innovative thinking, categorized in the three key areas of *creative thinking, strategic thinking,* and *transformational thinking*. This chapter contains more down-to-earth advice for stimulating innovation within the organizational setting.

By taking a systematic approach to innovation, new ideas can be created and moved through the system into application. The following discussion will help you design the optimal organizational environment, where everyone can be encouraged to take an active role in building an "innovation-centric" organization.

The Innovation Systems Architecture® Model

The Innovation Systems Architecture model was presented in Chapter 7. The model has been designed to be easily understood so that everyone can see how innovation can be implemented in all areas of the organization.

The model consists of eight key dimensions or *pillar*s that define the architecture for building and sustaining innovation. Thcsc pillars are:

1. Shared Innovation Vision and Strategy
2. Innovation Environment Supports
3. Innovation Resource Allocation
4. Innovation Process Networks
5. Innovation Programs
6. Innovation Skills Development
7. Innovation Rewards and Recognition
8. External Stakeholder Innovation (Customers and Partners)

Let's take a brief look at each of these pillars.

Pillar #1: Shared Innovation Vision and Strategy

Many employees think innovation is someone else's responsibility. "Let the research and development and marketing teams find new products to save the company. Let the sales team find new ways to satisfy our customers. It's not my job to find new ideas." In reality, a strong organization needs to encourage *everyone* to get into the trenches to look for and cultivate new ideas. Being at a certain level in the organizational chart or being in a specific department does not guarantee that the insights will be better than those of someone else. Indeed, new ideas can come from anywhere.

There is a well-known saying, "You get what you ask for." Many organizations list innovation as a core value in their mission statements and then fail to follow up with the necessary action steps to ensure that innovation does indeed become a rallying cry throughout the organization.

There are four steps in sharing an innovation vision and strategy:

1. Discuss what the concept of innovation means for your organization so that you can agree on a customized *definition of innovation.*

2. Develop an *innovation vision statement* for the organization. 3M created an innovation vision statement that says "We want to be the most

innovative organization," and then focused the entire organization on innovation. In her recent Speech from the Throne opening the first session of the 37th Parliament of Canada, Governor General Adrienne Clarkson announced that the Government of Canada would focus on building a world economy driven by innovation, ideas, and talent. "Our objective should be no less than to be recognized as one of the most innovative countries in the world."[1] Hewlett-Packard also focuses on innovation as a core vision and ensures that innovation is sought in every corner of the organization, from new-product development to sales and human-resource programs.

3. Develop an *innovation strategy* for integrating your organization's diverse innovation activities so that the overall goal of innovation can be supported. Ensure that your organization's activities and plans are linked to the overall vision and strategic priorities.

4. Communicate that innovation is an organizational goal and that everyone is encouraged to participate in developing their own, as well as the organization's, innovation capacity. To be effective, the innovation vision and strategy must be shared with all levels of the organization so that everyone has a chance to understand and participate in the organization's innovation agenda.

Pillar #2: Innovation Environment Supports

One of the biggest influences on innovation is the innovation environment, which either encourages or damages innovation efforts. The innovation environment is created by actual practices and behaviors, not simply by statements of "principles and policies" of what an innovation environment could be like.

Unfortunately, many employees feel isolated from other areas of the organization, including management, especially when it comes to submitting ideas and voicing concerns. According to Watson Wyatt, a comparison between management responses from the 1999 Innovation Survey and employee feedback from WorkSingapore revealed that "senior executives' intentions and actions may be perceived very differently by employees." Employers generally think they are very receptive, but employees tend to disagree.[2]

Even though everyone has a lot to offer, comments like "My ideas don't count. I'm just the low man on the totem pole," "They don't ask for my ideas so I don't bother sharing them," and "I'm new here so they don't think I know anything!" are heard too frequently. What a waste of resources. What a shame to miss out on potentially useful, if not revolutionary, ideas just because the person wasn't in the "right position" within the organization or her length of service or tenure within the organization was not considered "long enough." In order to stimulate a strong innovation environment, *everyone* must understand how they can contribute, and *everyone* must be encouraged to take an active role in offering new ideas.

The very acts of asking for innovation, reviewing innovative outcomes, and rewarding attempts as well as successes can serve not only as powerful motivators for your current employees but also as key strategies in attracting high-quality recruits. Southwest Airlines positions the employee as the number one priority. Its philosophy is that, if the employee is inspired, that inspiration will rub off on the customer who, in turn, will generate profits for the company and the shareholders. Other organizations seem to put shareholders first, customers second, and employees third.

Employees want to be treated as important members of the team and kept informed. Innovative organizations spend as much time communicating formally with employees as they do with the investment community! They share upcoming programs as well as keeping the learning alive within the organization via storytelling, videos, the Intranet, formal reviews, and reward ceremonies. An open style is encouraged so that ideas can travel freely from one team member to another and to other teams within the organization.

A strong innovation climate is one in which employees feel free to challenge each other and experiment with alternative approaches. Diversity of thought is embraced authentically. Employees who challenge the sacred traditions are supported and not treated as troublemakers. As an innovation leader, you must create a safe environment where people feel free to explore and experiment and are not afraid of being punished for "coloring outside the lines," especially if their objectives were admirable.

It is important that leaders be directly involved in innovation initiatives so that their commitment to innovation can be seen throughout the organization. The leader needs to be passionate about innovation and inspire the rest of the team, and, vice versa, the team must inspire the leader.

It is important to note that an innovation leader's job is not to build consensus for everything. Stopping to build consensus is too slow, if not impossible, for today's fast-paced economy. Instead, collaborative innovation where ideas are developed based on collective experience and a shared knowledge base enables decision-makers to retain the responsibility of choosing among the various options and to move the process forward.

In building a strong innovation environment, consider identifying and removing the barriers to innovative thinking and create a safe environment in which exploration and experimentation are encouraged.

Pillar #3: Innovation Resource Allocation

Many organizations have the resources to fund more innovative efforts but are risk-averse and hide behind financial hurdles or processes that serve to protect the status quo and slow down the innovation process.

Without adequate resources such as time, people, information, and financial support, the vision of becoming an innovative organization will not be realized. Consider widening the access to innovation resources in the following ways:

1. Allowing more time for the innovation process, especially during the early phase of exploring new opportunities and ideas.

2. Allowing more time for innovation champions to lead and coordinate their team's innovation efforts.

3. Redesigning the planning and budget processes to allow for more flexibility in funding the investigation, development, and implementation of new ideas.

4. Widening the access to capital, especially for ideas in the seed phase. We can learn from organizations like Dupont, where any employee can submit an entrepreneurial idea and seek funding for its development through the company's innovative $EED program.[3]

Pillar #4: Innovation Process Networks

One of the biggest challenges facing any organization is developing its procedures to identify, develop, and implement innovative ideas quickly. Innovation Process Networks are what hold an organization together and, as such, need to be strengthened to produce better innovation results. Analyze the strengths and weaknesses of your current processes. Where are the roadblocks in *identifying, developing,* and then *implementing* great ideas in a speedy manner?

According to a recent study conducted by Arthur Anderson, 67 percent of organizations did not have a formal process for gathering ideas.[4] Any organization can benefit from broadening its source of new ideas. Unless an organization has an idea-capture system, it is missing out on the opportunity to learn from the past and avoid repeating mistakes. Begin by asking for and accessing files that contain historical strategies, plans, and results. Set up processes to access information about your industry, including competitor profiles. Keep an eye on the changing marketplace and the evolving needs of your target customers. What processes do you have in place to detect early warning signs of changes in the marketplace? How are your opportunity-finding teams sharing what they learn?

Adding some structure to your idea-gathering processes does not have to represent added bureaucracy in your organization. The increased flow of comments and ideas should add positive energy to your organization, not result in more dead-end paperwork or wasted effort.

Establish cross-functional or cross-organizational group idea-sharing forums to share ideas and fresh perspectives. Establish processes to solicit new ideas via suggestion programs. "Japanese companies make it a point to solicit and reward suggestions on how to improve operations from employees. The Nissan Motor factory . . . rewards each and every idea suggested . . . depending on its value when adopted. Japanese workers overall make an average of 24 suggestions to their companies per year, ten times the rate in the United States."[5]

These suggestion programs must include a review process. Organizations that simply set up a Web site or database so that teams and others can contribute ideas often end up being disappointed with the results. Employees are often reluctant to submit their great suggestions because they don't understand what will happen to their ideas, how their ideas will be evaluated, how much time it will take to evaluate them, and how they might be rewarded for participating. Most people want recognition for submitting their ideas, and they want to know that the process is supported by senior managers who can potentially approve the implementation of their ideas. As the old adage says, "You can lead a horse to water but you can't make him drink." If you are contemplating establishing an idea database, don't overlook the basic human needs for belonging and recognition.

In terms of idea development, there are many effective approaches. The managers at Royal Dutch/Shell encouraged the submission of ideas using a combination of their Intranet, brainstorming days, and pitches to approval panels. Idea teams had the opportunity to pitch their new ideas to a management panel; if the idea was deemed valuable, the team would be encouraged to develop it further and then receive funding. Up to 30 percent of their research and development ventures were funded from this process with the amount of funding ranging from $100,000 to $600,000.[6]

General Electric is well known for its three-day Workout Sessions where employees, suppliers, and sometimes customers, work on problems for two days without the presence of their supervisors. On the third day, the supervisor listens to the proposal and responds immediately with the recommended next steps. The type of ideas developed during the Workout Sessions may include ideas to cut unnecessary work as well as improve processes, cycle time, and communication. This approach conveys a sense of urgency for solving these challenges as well as providing a good forum for the participants to focus their efforts.[7]

Employees at Nortel Networks were granted a small amount of funding to develop proposals for their new ideas. These proposals were then taken to the venture investment board and if approved, received full funding.[8] Other organizations build cross-functional innovation teams to look at and build ideas. Employees are asked to submit their ideas to the idea-advocate groups who, in turn, review the ideas against pre-established criteria and convert the chosen ideas into stronger proposals. The idea-advocate groups or idea agents then take the strongest ideas to the management team for review. It is important, if these idea advocates are going to represent the larger groups' ideas, that they have training in idea development and selection.

Don't let ideas get caught up in red tape. Develop processes that will allow ideas to reach top management, as well as processes that provide for the incubation of new ideas until they have a chance to develop. Remember that the objectives of any idea-creation and development process are twofold: (1) to identify strong ideas and (2) to motivate employees to participate.

If you want to be innovative, you must accelerate your idea-gathering and decision-making processes. Consider:

1. *Using technology, both online and offline.* Process technology such as that offered by Emmperative.com can be very beneficial in keeping the team on track during the development process. Enterprise management systems are also beneficial.

2. *Pushing decision-making down to the level at which it is most efficient.* Waiting for approvals is one of the largest time wasters in idea development, especially if managers tend to be on different vacation schedules! You do not want things grinding to a halt just because someone is on a ski trip in Taos or sunning themselves in Tahiti.

3. *Using parallel processing techniques so that you are not waiting for task A to finish before starting task B.* The traditional sequential approach to idea development wastes too much time. For example, Microsoft employs a large development team that divides into small teams that work independently but then connect at certain milestones in the development process to discuss progress and options for the subsequent phases. The team attempts to do everything in parallel with frequent synchronizations. This loose but organized structure allows for flexibility in design while pursuing a common vision.[9]

The innovation process is not linear. Make sure you leave room for flexibility in your processes to accommodate changes in direction. Some processes, such as some well-known new-product development processes, are so tight that they do not leave enough room for experimentation or looping back to previous stages.

You must also consider who is going to develop the idea. You will need to investigate the relative merits of development in-house, by special team (or skunkworks), by a partner organization, by a specialized incubator organization, or just spinning it off early and leaving development to the purchaser of the idea. All five options are valid depending on the resources—talent, time, funding—available to the original creator of the idea. One word of caution: Consider the human as well as the resource implications and requirements of bringing an idea back into the mainstream organization if it was developed outside.

The third and final area to consider comprises the processes for idea implementation. Once the idea has been developed into a full business plan and approvals have been granted, strong project-management processes are needed for the speedy and effective implementation of the idea. Depending on the scope of the project, a collaborative innovation team will be needed to support the timelines, resource requirements, and course corrections needed for the launch of the idea as well as for the ongoing support of the idea in Year One, Year Two, Year Three, etc. The process must also consider the course corrections that will be needed, especially if the idea is not well received either internally within the organization or externally in the marketplace.

It is also important to share stories of the ideas that were implemented and what was achieved. A FedEx Custom Critical team posts their "wow stories" on the company's Intranet, and each week the team votes for the best example of innovation. By posting the stories on the Intranet, the entire team benefits from learning what has worked and participates in rewarding innovation in action.

Innovation process networks can help the team work together to reduce the barriers between departments and promote the innovative spirit throughout the organization. Consider what process networks your team or organization uses for idea generation, idea development, and idea implementation. Then consider designing innovation into the existing processes—budgeting, operations, planning, new-product development, and information processes. Where these processes are ineffective, design a new one.

Pillar #5: Innovation Programs

An innovation program is designed specifically to focus everyone's attention on improving and sustaining innovation. It is a campaign with a designated starting and finishing time. Examples of effective innovation-suggestion programs include Southwest Airlines, which holds campaigns to generate new ideas in certain areas; and W. L. Gore & Associates, best known for its GORE-TEX fabrics, where suggestions programs are used regularly to encourage everyone to keep their eyes and ears open for new ideas, including those that may be outside their direct work area or scope of responsibility. It should come as no surprise that both of these companies are among *Fortune* magazine's 2001 ranking of the "100 Best Companies to Work For" in America. Other examples of innovation programs are:

- The Development Marketplace held annually at the World Bank Group to showcase innovative projects in economic and community development.

- The Breakfast of Innovation champions program, sponsored by Hewlett-Packard.

- The Ideas in AAction Program, sponsored by American Airlines, which went beyond the simple "suggestion box" idea to represent a full innovation program focused on finding savings or profit improvements. The program resulted in savings of $83 million.[10]

Pillar #6: Innovation Skills Development

Innovative thinking is a skill that can be taught and that, with practice, can be improved. It is critical that members of the team feel confident in finding, developing, and implementing new ideas in order to maximize their own, as well as the organization's, innovation capacity. Both Xerox and Frito-Lay, through their respective Gain Sharing programs, embarked on innovative-thinking training for thousands of their employees. Other organizations have implemented three-day innovative-thinking training with the objective of developing a common language and approach to innovation within the organization. Some organizations engage speakers to spark the creative energies of their employees while others encourage employees to post one-page summaries of their innovative activities on the Intranet for shared learning.

Consider designing and implementing an innovation-skills development program with the objective of developing innovation as a core competency throughout the organization. Boost everyone's confidence in finding and developing innovative ideas by including training elements such as:

1. Creative-thinking training so that everyone is taught to notice trends, look for alternative approaches, and make new connections.

2. Strategic-thinking training so that everyone has the basic skills to develop a creative idea into a strategic one that can bring value to the organization. An understanding of the commercialization process is critical to all members of the organization, especially those in the research and development function.

3. Transformational-thinking training so that everyone can become more aware of the interconnectivity of their attitudes and behaviors and can find new ways to support innovation throughout the organization.

Pillar #7: Innovation Rewards and Recognition

Although the call for innovation presumes that people are ready and willing to stretch into new territory and even break rules, many organizations reward the opposite, the protection of the status quo. It is important to set innovation as a performance objective for everyone, regardless of position or department. Make sure each manager discusses and sets an innovation objective for each and every member of the team.

Recognize both individual and group efforts through informal recognition, celebration dinners, and prizes. Southwest Airlines, for instance, makes celebrating part of their culture and, therefore, employees feel respected and valued. 3M chronicles success stories and shares these stories widely across the organization. Harris Scientific holds Achievement Day celebrations.[11] Milliken & Company has a Hall of Innovators where it profiles pictures of innovators and descriptions of their innovations.[12] Other organizations distribute monthly videos profiling winners of continuous improvement programs, as well as highlighting them in internal publications. Still others use their Intranet, random cash rewards, personalized letters from the president, and "Super Innovation Team" awards. Other companies recognize individuals on development teams, such as scientists or product line employees, in corporate advertisements. Be innovative with your reward and recognition programs. Instead of the once-a-year bonus, why not offer random cash rewards or perhaps rewards every four months? This may also be more in line with the trend toward instant gratification in many other areas of life.

There is, however, also evidence that suggests not putting too much emphasis on the reward. Alfie Kohn, in his book *Punished by Rewards*, argues that people might become so focused on the reward that they lose site of the overall objective, including their passion for the actual work.[13] In this regard, establishing sales contests between regions might also be detrimental to innovation. By setting one team against another within your organization, you are establishing the conditions that, as Kohn says, "others become the obstacle to my success." One team might not share its great ideas—for example, how it found a better way to attract new customers or sell through a new distribution channel—with other teams for fear of sharing its strategy for winning the internally focused sales contest.

Pillar #8: External Stakeholder Innovation

All too often, organizations rely primarily on ideas generated internally instead of capitalizing on ideas from both inside and outside the organization. In addition to broadening their perspective via the Internet, research reports, and tradeshows, each innovation team should connect with teams outside its organization to form a community of extended stakeholders, including customers, suppliers, regulatory agencies, other partners, and even competitors. This is similar to the concept of the magnetwork, which was introduced in Chapter 6. Here are some suggestions for strengthening your magnetwork:

1. Create alliances with the players at the beginning of the design and production process. Work with them to shorten product-development cycles, cut costs, and capitalize on technological breakthroughs. Chrysler, Ford, and Toyota, for example, all use an extended enterprise of suppliers and benefit from bringing them in at the beginning of the design process so that they can gain a deeper understanding of the project and contribute additional expertise.[14] Technology firms such as Lucent and Sun Microsystems also view their suppliers as key players in filling competency gaps and accelerating time to market. Sun Microsystems has worked with its suppliers to streamline product development and dramatically reduce costs.[15] University and industry representatives are also increasing their knowledge-sharing and collaboration partnerships.

2. Create alliances with the players at the implementation and follow-up phases of the process. Work with them to develop more innovative ways to find and service customers. FedEx partners with ground transportation companies who deliver the courier package to the end customer while FedEx retains control of their well-known brand and their highly developed proprietary technology system.

3. Create alliances with other organizations that may be offering products or services similar to yours. Hewlett-Packard, for example, purchased the engine for its line of laser jet printers from Canon. Financial institutions that use the VISA brand name outsource the processing of their VISA transactions to other financial institutions, thus allowing them to offer this essential service to their customers at a lower cost.

Other examples of collaborative innovation are the many international networks that have formed as a result of the proliferation of the Internet—networks like Entovation.com, founded by Debra Amidon to focus on advancing the understanding of Knowledge Management and Innovation, and the Innovation Network, founded by Joyce Wycoff, focused on advancing shared learning on innovation. These kinds of network structures provide a platform for collaborative action that is just beginning to be recognized.

Consider strengthening your external stakeholder innovation by:

1. Sharing ideas and best practices with other organizations and agencies.

2. Inviting more participation from your external stakeholders. Sponsor collaborative innovation-planning sessions with partners, suppliers, and customers to identify new ideas.

3. Designing and implementing a process to gather input from your external stakeholders.

4. Rewarding and recognizing this input for mutual benefit.

The Innovative Organization Assessment: A Holistic Approach©

Before an organization can determine how it is going to improve its capacity for innovation, it must first determine how well the organization is currently doing in terms of innovation. One area of measurement is called *innovation output.* Organizations often measure their innovation output in terms of new product success, such as the number of patents granted or the percentage of revenue, profit, and/or market share that can be attributed to new products launched in the last year or some other period of time. Others tend to quantify their innovation output in terms of overall improvements in profit margins, bottomline profit, cost reductions, and reductions in cycle time to launch new initiatives. Still other methods include gauging the improvement in ratings in customer satisfaction, ratings of organizational image by independent reviewers, and ranking in terms of attractiveness of the organization for new hires or employee retention.

The other area of measurement is called *innovation throughput.* This looks at how well the organization has established the design or infrastructure to support innovation on a continuous basis. Drawing an analogy to automobiles, *innovation output* represents how many miles per gallon (or liter) the car achieved, while *innovation throughput* represents how well the engine was designed to produce the best mileage output.

To measure innovation throughput, one can look holistically at the eight pillars of the Innovation Systems Architecture model just presented. Based on this model, my colleague Alex Pattakos and I developed an assessment instrument called *The Innovative Organization Assessment: A Holistic Approach* (IOA), published and distributed worldwide by HRDQ. The assessment was developed by reverse engineering the key components of innovation that were found in organizations producing innovative products or services. An extensive literature search, as well as results from a wide variety of practical field-tested experiences, contributed additional perspective and was used to increase the rigor of the assessment product.

Besides providing a quantifiable measure of the extent to which a team or organizational group possesses the capacity for holistic innovation, the IOA also provides a process by which participants can deepen their awareness and understanding of how innovation could positively impact the organization. We designed the IOA to serve multiple purposes:

- To provide a common framework for describing and understanding innovation. The assesssment questions and participant workbook provide a simple, easy-to-understand appproach to innovation.

- To provide a way to define and measure the organizational design or infrastructure needed to cultivate and sustain innovation.

- To provide a series of metrics that can be used to benchmark innovation capacity within a team or across the entire organization. The metrics can be used to make comparisons between teams within the same organization as well as between the organization and our normative IOA database. These metrics can be obtained on a one-time basis or repeated over time to measure improvements in innovation capacity.

- To provide practical, results-oriented action steps to build your organization's innovation capacity. The data generated from the assessment process provides an excellent diagnosis of strong and weak areas. Through discussion, the team can pinpoint areas for improvement.

A more extensive explanation of the Innovation Systems Architecture model and the *Innovative Organization Assessment: A Holistic Approach* is available from the authors or through HRDQ.com.

CHAPTER 11

Conclusion

There is a commonly held view that innovation is the same as creativity. This is not the case. Creativity can be defined as "the discovery of a new idea or connection." I have suggested that 98 percent of ideas already exist somewhere in the universe. Creative thinking is about finding these ideas and connecting them in a new way. But innovation is much more than just finding and connecting these creative ideas. It is about strategy and action—bringing value to the organization through the implementation of these creative and strategic ideas. Innovation can therefore be defined as "the profitable implementation of strategic creativity."

There is another commonly held view that innovation is associated with new products, new technology, and the research and development team. This view is too limiting. As we have seen, innovation can be applied broadly across all elements of the organization, such as existing products, services, programs, processes, and business models.

Finally, there is a commonly held view that the concepts of efficiency and innovation are diametrically opposed. Using the Innovation Value Continuum, we can see that efficiency ideas, or ideas that provide marginal improvements to existing products, services, and programs, are, in fact, a part of the overall concept of innovation. All new ideas, whether they pertain to Efficiency Innovation (marginal improvements to what already exists), Evolutionary Innovation (distinctly new and better ideas), or Revolutionary Innovation (radically new and better ideas), are needed by all organizations.

The challenge for most organizations is to balance the pursuit of these three types of innovation. If the organization pursues too much Efficiency Innovation and is too focused on improving the productivity of what already exists, it runs the risk of missing opportunities in the marketplace. If the organization pursues too much Revolutionary Innovation, it runs the risk of throwing the organization into a state of chaos and also disenfranchising those employees who do not have the mindset or the skill base to identify and pursue radically new changes in direction. In reality, Revolutionary Innovation may only be a realistic objective for a very small percentage of organizations and a very small percentage of employees within these organizations. For most organizations, their realistic challenge is to move from too much Efficiency Innovation to a greater emphasis on Evolutionary Innovation. This is particularly true for capital-intensive organizations that have a tendency to return to perfecting what they already do and who also have a tendency to discount new ideas if they do not fit with existing return on investment financial hurdles.

The Seeds of Innovation

The unique approach to innovative thinking presented in this book involves the integration of three competency areas: *creative thinking, strategic thinking,* and *transformational thinking.*

The Seeds of Creative Thinking

Creative thinking involves leaving the known and entering the unknown. It is about burning new neural connections in the brain so that creative ideas have the opportunity to surface. Many people stop themselves from experiencing new things and only want to stay in their comfort zones that reinforce "the right way." Often, they seek out more order and control despite knowing that mastering order and control in today's world is a formidable and perhaps unattainable challenge.

Many people stop themselves from being creative because they do not believe in their ability to be creative. The first principle of creative thinking is: *Believe in creativity.* Believe in the creative talents of everyone. Celebrate everyone's unique approach to creative thinking.

The second principle is: *Be curious.* Great creative thinkers have an insatiable appetite for understanding how things work and for connecting new thoughts with old ones. They feel free to challenge their own assumptions and those of others. They make room for new ideas by unlearning or forgetting some of what they thought to be true. They know that creativity requires a new mindset. They ask probing questions and listen to the answers they receive with open minds. They seek out diverse stimuli so that they can see more options and find more connections.

The third principle of creative thinking is: *Discover new connections.* Most ideas already exist in some form somewhere in the universe—in some other department, organization, industry sector, or country. Finding these ideas and then experimenting to mix and match or cut and paste them into new ideas is the essence of creative thinking. Learning how to connect or cross-fertilize ideas into new ones using the Creative-Connections Powertools will greatly increase a person's creative thinking skills.

The Seeds of Strategic Thinking

Strategy is really about connecting creativity with value. Strategic-thinking decisions are based on (a) an understanding of customers' current and emerging needs; (b) an understanding of the organization's current and anticipated future core competencies (special skills or knowledge), resources, and culture; and (c) a future view of the industry sector or marketplace.

The first principle of strategic thinking is: *See the BIG Picture.* Systems thinking is about looking at the whole entity, not just the parts. Importantly, it is about looking at the *relationship* between the parts and the whole, and understanding the effect a change on one part will have on the other parts. It is important to see how everything is related—from the projects to the teams to the organization to the marketplace and even to the future marketplace. Great innovators also see the BIG Picture by spending time defining the Real Problem as a way to avoid heading off in too many directions. They use Innovation Goalposts to guide the identification of high-value ideas and set realistic expectations. They also predetermine the criteria for these high-value ideas using the Six BIG-Picture criteria.

The ability to recognize value in things that other people do not see sets innovators apart. Those who focus on the current structure of the market are falling behind those who focus on creating the future, changing the rules of the game, and creating stronger value. The second principle of strategic thinking is: *Look to the future*. In order to do so, innovators must explore the patterns and opportunities in the strategic landscape and then develop a vision of what they want to be or what they want to be famous for. From here, the various ways to evolve the organization toward this vision can be discussed.

The third principle of strategic thinking is: *Do the extraordinary*. Great innovators can evolve from the ordinary to the extraordinary by using the following nine strategies:

1. Target the most profitable customer.
2. Offer something distinctly new and better.
3. Set your innovation priorities.
4. Make sure it's easy.
5. Pick up the pace.
6. Systemize with modules.
7. Profit from the power of branding.
8. Add credibility.
9. Create magnetworks.

Strategic thinking is really the ability to marry creative ideas with the needs of the organization and the marketplace. To do so, everyone must balance his or her view of the internal organization with that of the external marketplace. They must balance their view of today as well as the future.

The Seeds of Transformational Thinking

Transformational thinking pertains to both the intrapersonal and interpersonal aspects of innovation. Often, what is stopping innovation is not the lack of a creative or strategic idea but the attitudinal and behavioral barriers placed in front of it, either by individuals or collectively by the team. Awareness of these barriers is the first step in understanding how to address them so that innovative efforts—from idea conception to implementation—can be supported.

The first principle of transformational thinking is: *Seek greater awareness.* This is about shifting the mental models so that people see the bigger picture of their personal interactions with others. It begins with an awareness of oneself and others as well as an awareness of the interaction between oneself and others. To quote NBA coach Phil Jackson from his book *Sacred Hoops,* sometimes "it is more important to be aware than it is to be smart."[1] In addition to understanding oneself, it is important to understand the team dynamics as well as the organizational design that can provide the fertile environment in which innovative ideas can grow.

Often innovative efforts are blocked by a lack of passion. So many people have lost the passion for what they do, which effectively limits their contributions to themselves, their team, and their total organization. People can lose their passion if they hear too many Passion Killers such as "We've tried that before," "We haven't tried that before," "That wasn't invented here," and "The boss will never approve that." We all need to hear more Passion Supports such as "You're right on track" and "That's a great idea."

Innovation requires passionate people who can bring life to ideas. Just as a saxophone is nothing without air, great ideas are nothing without the passionate people who develop and support them. The second principle of transformational thinking is: *Ignite passion.* Innovation comes not only from the mind but also from the heart and soul. Innovators need to tap into their own source of passion as well as unleash the innovative spirit among others. They need the courage to speak up and be comfortable with being the odd one out when offering a new perspective.

Whereas certain environments can definitely bring out the passionate spirit in people, others can definitely kill this passionate spirit. Understanding the characteristics of these innovative as well as non-innovative environments is important for building your capacity in transformational thinking. Often leaders send mixed messages—they ask for innovation but then shut it down when someone threatens the status quo with a new perspective. This is the crux of the innovation challenge. Innovation is about doing something distinctly new and better, but in order to be able to embrace innovation, one must be willing to be uncomfortable for a while. Challenging the status quo often leads to tension and sometimes to conflict. Unfortunately, many people are not comfortable with conflict and, as a result, retreat back into doing what they've always done.

The third principle of transformational thinking is: *Take action*. If ideas are not accepted and implemented, the value of having these ideas cannot be realized. In order to capitalize upon their potential, it is important that ideas be packaged and presented in a way that maximizes their understanding and acceptance. Developing these ideas and the Innovation Roadmap includes categorizing the new ideas according to their potential, checking the ideas against the Six BIG-Picture criteria and Innovation Goalposts, and then writing the plan. It is the responsibility of the innovator to prepare the idea for the audience and the audience for the idea. In order to gain commitment to the idea, an innovator must first understand what the needs of the audience are and be willing to repackage the idea to maximize the chances of acceptance.

Implementing the plan is never a smooth process. Even if it means taking three steps forward, two steps sideways, and one step back, be persistent in order to gain forward movement toward your goal. Above all, be patient. It takes time to find support for any idea and overcome others' resistance to change. Just as the seasons change, you must be willing to accommodate the ambiguities that flow naturally from any harvesting process.

Organizational Innovation

Transformational thinking also involves a heightened awareness of interdependency vis-à-vis the team and the total organization. Every organization needs an environment where innovation can flourish. So often leaders ask people to "think outside the box," yet they design the organizations to consistently put them back in the box!

We need to look at how innovation capacity can be encouraged and developed on a sustained basis. Build an "innovation-centric" organization in order to capitalize upon the wealth of ideas that does exist and can exist within the organization. Find a way to bring new ideas to the surface and get them through the system and out into the marketplace.

The Innovation Systems Architecture® model provides a framework in which we can see areas where innovation can be encouraged throughout the organization.

Attending to each of the eight pillars of the model will ensure that innovation is seen as a priority throughout the organization. Of course, one size does not fit all. The design and implementation of the elements of the Innovation Systems Architecture must be customized to fit the unique needs of your particular organization.

The Interrelationship

What is especially important to note is the interrelationship between the building blocks or seeds of *creative thinking, strategic thinking*, and *transformational thinking*. Although these seeds were presented as distinct, they are not independent of each other. The interrelationship between these can be illustrated by the following:

- Believing in creativity (Chapter 1) so you can ignite passion in yourself and others (Chapter 8)
- Being willing to unlearn and forget (Chapter 1) and recognize our sacred traditions (Chapter 2)
- Being curious and having an open mind (Chapter 2) in order to gain new insights for the future (Chapter 5)
- Gaining a different perspective (Chapter 2) by seeing the BIG Picture (Chapter 4)
- Asking probing questions (Chapter 2) to order to find new trends (Chapter 5)
- Discovering new connections and using your imagination (Chapter 3) in order to plan for the future (Chapter 5)
- Finding diverse stimuli (Chapter 3) by broadening your Innovation Radar Screen (Chapter 5)
- Taking a systems-thinking approach (Chapter 4) in order to develop the organizational system to support innovation (Chapter 10)

■ Clarifying the Real Problem (Chapter 4) before using the Creative-Connections Powertools (Chapter 3)

■ Setting Innovation Goalposts (Chapter 4) so that preparing and presenting innovative ideas is easier (Chapter 9)

■ Seeking greater awareness (Chapter 7) in order to ignite passion (Chapter 8)

■ Using the Nine Strategies for Becoming Extraordinary (Chapter 6) before taking action (Chapter 9)

As you can see, the Seeds of Innovation presented in this book are truly interrelated. In this case, 1+1 equals more than 2. Taking a holistic view of innovation produces more than the sum of the parts.

Summary

Gone are the days when one person or one department could be focused on the future while everyone else kept their heads down and focused on the present. Leaders now know that they need to have every employee in every area of the organization be on the lookout for innovative ideas. They now know that they need an Innovation Roadmap and detailed action plans in order to help their teams and organization support innovation on a continuous basis.

But "innovation is not 'flash of genius'. It's hard work."[2] It is hard work to move people away from their sacred traditions and their propensity to conform to industry norms. It is hard work to get people to admit that what they are doing today is not working any more. It is hard work to get people to drop their emotional attachment to "the way we do things around here" and take the leap to a new way. And it is hard work to stay the course and confront the natural tendency for people to return to their old and comfortable way of doing things.

Use the insights and guidance provided in this book to develop your own capacity for innovative thinking. Use the book to develop the Innovation Roadmap needed to enable your organization to become a leading "innovation-centric" organization. In the spirit of the famous innovator, Walt Disney, "Dream. Believe. Dare. Do."[3]

APPENDIX A

The Nine-Step Innovation Process

The Nine-Step Innovation Process calls for alternating exploratory and concentrated thinking at each step. In this regard, exploratory thinking includes expanding thinking to look for new ideas, withholding judgment, accepting all possibilities, and looking for a quantity of ideas through new connections. In contrast, concentrated thinking includes contracting thinking to be more direct, making judgments and evaluating options, and looking for quality in line with overall strategic objectives.

There are three stages, understanding, imagination, and action, with three steps in each stage.

The Nine-Step Innovation Process

STEP	EXPLORATION	CONCENTRATION
UNDERSTANDING		
Step 1	**1- A**	**1- B**
GATHERING INFORMATION	Choose the team that will address the problem. Explore the dynamics behind what the team thinks is the problem. Gather facts, opinions, and details from different perspectives. Apply "who/what/where/why/how/when" to the problem. Explore the external marketplace for more information.	Analyze the problem and choose the best information, which helps you and your team to understand the problem better.
Step 2	**2-A**	**2-B**
CLARIFYING THE REAL PROBLEM	Broaden awareness and clarification of the problem. Identify and list the likely causes of the problem. Draft options for the "problem statements."	Choose the "problem statement" that best describes what is believed to be the most significant or real problem.
Step 3	**3-A**	**3-B**
SETTING INNOVATION GOALPOSTS	Explore the range of acceptability for options and solutions for this particular problem and explore important decision-making criteria. Review the Six BIG-Picture criteria.	Set the Innovation Goalposts.
IMAGINATION		
Step 4	**4-A**	**4-B**
SEEKING STIMULI	Explore the environment for signals and other information. Research past, present, and future. Explore multiple perspectives. Explore the marketplace.	Analyze and narrow down the stimuli.

STEP	EXPLORATION	CONCENTRATION
Step 5	**5-A**	**5-B**
UNCOVERING INSIGHTS	Use your chosen stimuli and imagination to identify potential insights and discoveries. Suspend judgment while you are uncovering these insights. Use the Creative-Connections Powertools.	Choose the high-priority insights for further reflection.
Step 6	**6-A**	**6-B**
IDENTIFYING IDEAS	Explore these high-priority insights for potential ideas to solve your real problem.	Compare and select the best ideas based on the previously discussed Innovation Goalposts. Build these ideas into fuller concepts.
ACTION		
Step 7	**7-A**	**Step 7-B**
DEVELOPING THE INNOVATION ROADMAP	Take these concepts and build them into fuller plans. Investigate resource needs, timing, and responsibilities. Identify alternative plans.	Choose the optimal plan based on the Innovation Goalposts and predetermined criteria. Consider the impact this plan will have on the rest of the organization.
Step 8	**8-A**	**8-B**
GAINING COMMITMENT	Explore commitment to the optimal plan. Identify who will support the plan. Prepare the plan for presentation.	Present the plan. Readjust the plan. Test elements of the plan if desired. Readjust the plan. Finalize commitment to the final plan.
Step 9	**9-A**	**9-B**
IMPLEMENTING THE INNOVATION ROADMAP	Release the final plan into action. Adjust the plan where needed.	Review the entire process and results, and share this learning.

APPENDIX B

List of Probing Questions

Here is a list of probing questions that will aid you in becoming more curious!

- Who recommended this plan?
- Why did they recommend it?
- What else did they look at?
- Who is affected by this plan?
- What is the cost to implement this plan over the next five years?
- Who is the target market for this product?
- Why do they buy this product?
- What other products are similar?
- What makes this product better than the other products?

- What is wrong with our product?
- Who uses this service?
- Why do they use this service?
- Who doesn't use this service? Why not?
- When do they use this service?
- When do they not use this service?
- Why do we have so many defects?
- Where are the bottlenecks?
- What inventory levels do we really need?
- Why does it take so long to get the information we need?
- How are we scheduling our time?
- Why do all the ads in our category look the same?
- Do our customers understand our advertising?
- Are we communicating our position in an easy-to-understand manner?
- Why are we advertising?
- Do we need to advertise?
- Should we advertise when our product isn't the best?
- Have any new products in our category been successful?
- Are older products, when improved, more successful than new ones?
- In what regions of the country are new products more successful? Why?
- What customer groups are buying the new product?
- Why would anyone want to work at our company or agency?

- What other options do they have?
- In what ways is our company a better place to work than others?
- What are we offering our employees that other companies aren't?
- Why would people support this program?
- Is it the best program?
- What are the other emerging issues that need to be addressed by this program?

APPENDIX C

Ninety-Nine Innovations

Use the following list of innovations as stimuli for generating new ideas. Look at what might have been "combined or connected" in order to create this innovation.

Be inspired by the inventors of these innovations, who had to persevere when they faced opposition to "the way it's always been done."

99 INNOVATIVE INNOVATIONS	What might have been "combined" or "connected" in order to create this innovation?
Air conditioning	
Airbag	
Airplane	
Alcohol	
Alphabet	
Amusement parks	
Artificial blood	
Artificial organs	

Automatic teller machine
Automobiles
Auto-pilot
Battery
Bluetooth convergence technology
Boat
Books
Braille
Brakes
Calculators
Calendar
Central heating
Cereal
Clock
CNN
Coffee
Compact disk
Computer
Computer chip
Computer mouse
Corrective lenses
Courier service
Credit card
De-icing for airplanes
Dentistry
Deodorant
Diapers
Dishwasher
Distance learning
Dry cleaning
Elections
Electricity
Elevator
Fast food
Fax machine
Fingerprints

Flex hours
Frisbee
Hair dye
Highways
Income tax system
Internet
Judicial system
Lightbulb
Maps
Marriage
Mass production
Mathematics
Microwave
Mirror
Motorcycle
Movies
MTV
Paper
Parachute
Passport
Pharmaceuticals
Photocopying
Photography
Plaster cast for broken bones
Police services
Postal service
Printing press
Radio
Refrigeration
Remote control
Seatbelts
Shoes
Shopping mall
Soap
Spell checker
Stock market

Surgery
Telephone
Telescope
Television
Toilet
Toothpaste
Traffic light
Train
Vacations
Vacuum cleaner
Velcro
Vitamins
Voice activation
Voice recognition
Waste management
Water purification
Welfare system
Wheels on suitcases
Windshield wipers

APPENDIX D

Ninety-Nine Trends

Use the following list of trends as stimuli to increase your awareness of the BIG Picture and to look to the future. Review each trend and determine how it is applicable to your particular project or organization.

	TREND	IMPACT ON OUR ORGANIZATION OR PROJECT
1.	Acceptance and pursuit of global brands	
2.	Aesthetic appreciation—greater interest in the design of work and home environments	
3.	An increased need to define "seniors" by a division into groups: younger seniors (50 and 60) versus older seniors 70, 80, and 90	
4.	Antiglobalism—rebellion against organizations such as the World Trade Organization	
5.	Apathy of political systems—low voter turnout	
6.	Artificial intelligence	
7.	Biotechnology	

8.	Bluetooth convergence technology
9.	Branding of everything
10.	Breaking point for environmental shifts—more people are noticing excessive snow, rain, heat, earthquakes
11.	Commercialism of everything including education and medicine
12.	Consumer desire for low prices with online bargain shopping and interest in manufacturer/factory-direct-to-consumer shopping
13.	Copycat deviance with rebellion through youth riots, and use of such services as Napster
14.	Crisis in availability of natural resources. Water crisis, energy crisis
15.	Crisis in purpose in life after retirement. Issue with retirement being at age 55 and average life expectancy of 80, leaves 25 years of low productivity. Time for more reflection
16.	Crisis and potential bankruptcy in social security and pension funds with increase in aging population and fewer youth to support funds
17.	Demand for more information, right to know more
18.	Deregulated economy leading to more competition
19.	Desire for instant gratification
20.	Desire for more privacy
21.	Desire to look young forever. Interest in anti-aging therapy for both men and women
22.	Digital interactive television
23.	Display of aggression—road rage, air rage, parking-lot rage, store rage, school rage
24.	Distance learning, e-learning
25.	Employees wanting and demanding more participation in decision making
26.	Entertainment in everything—marrying entertainment with education, entertainment with sports
27.	Exploding quantity of and access to information
28.	Fear for security leading to more gated communities, car alarms, and martial arts instruction. Desire for more security everywhere—home, office, school, airplanes
29.	Feelings of detachment from others. Desire for more and deeper connections
30.	Genetic screening for all ages. Testing for diseases

31. Genetically modified food
32. Global positioning systems to locate anything, anywhere, anytime
33. Global shopping and purchasing via the Internet
34. Greed—increasing disparity between the haves and have nots
35. Growing concern for toxins in food, water, air, home. Concern for pesticides and contamination. Desire for more information and purity
36. Growing curiosity about Eastern culture, e.g. Zen, Feng Shui
37. Growing interest in experiences as a replacement for materialism
38. Growing interest in healthy food such as sushi, seaweed, and tofu
39. Health consciousness. Increasing interest in healthy unprocessed foods, organic foods. Also interest in alternative health care, natural cures
40. Impatience—demand for instant service, real time response, 24 hour service. Demand for speed. Everyone wants it "now"
41. Increase in home health care
42. Increase in illegal immigration
43. Increase in loyalty and frequent-purchaser programs
44. Increased interest in the shift to mind experiences and learning as the body ages
45. Increased fear of computer viruses and hackers. Desire for more computer security
46. Increased interest in educational standards and home schooling
47. Increased interest in nature and gardening
48. Increased job-hopping as company loyalty decreases
49. Increasing acceptance of massage as relaxation therapy, interest in yoga, easy exercise, tai chi
50. Increasing bandwidth, cost of bandwidth decreasing
51. Increasing choice of products and services, but too many options leading to more competition, and demand for lower prices
52. Increasing competitiveness and status consciousness of children, teens
53. Increasing connectivity through the Internet

54. Increasing interest in safe nature adventures

55. Increasing life expectancy as the result of breakthroughs in medicine, artificial body parts, cloning

56. Increasing penetration of computers and internet usage

57. Increasing usage of long distance calls via the Internet

58. Increasing variety of work structures and relationships. Work decentralization through technology

59. Individual rights—expectations of personal power, serve "me first"

60. Information workers—working 24 hours 7 days a week, accessible anywhere, anytime via technology

61. Interest in extreme sports and thrills

62. Interest in international culture for entertainment and food

63. Interest in tradition and nostalgia as a way to seek stability in a changing world

64. Laser technology

65. Less formality, less protocol, less regard for "the rules." Increased outspokenness—voice your opinion even if it is considered "rude"

66. Less international legal protection for patents, trademarks, etc.

67. Living vicariously via reality television, i.e. *Spy TV*, *Survivor*, *Fear Factor*

68. Loss of privacy. Digital cameras watching us everywhere

69. Loss of respect for traditional authority figures such as teachers, politicians, physicians

70. Mobile internet revolution—integration of data, internet, voice technology, through mobile phones. Growth of m-commerce

71. Nanotechnology—growing interest in the science of small

72. Networking—more collaboration with other organizations, industries, and countries

73. Increase in online banking and financial services

74. Paparazzi—no limits for overzealous journalists

75. PDAs (personal digital assistants)

76. Increase in pet ownership and dollars spent on pets

77. Proliferation of motorized wheelchairs with the aging population

78. Quick fix wanted for everything—for diets, relationships, spirituality, desire to feel good quickly

79. Quick sabbaticals, mini vacations for rejuvenation, spa get-aways

80. Rapid introduction of new technology. Need for more technical support as technology becomes prevalent and more complicated

81. Rebellion against excessive wealth, particularly salaries of executive managers earning 100 times the salary of entry level employees

82. Rebellion against majority rule. Minority groups want more and more special rights

83. Redesigned products and services for elderly, less mobile customers

84. Scarcity of skilled employees

85. Smart buildings, smart homes, smart appliances, smart cards—computer chip in everything, high tech offices and homes

86. Street-smart children

87. Tax revolt caused by fewer younger people (wage earners) supporting more older people (retirees)

88. Technology breakthroughs and more applications for voice recognition and eye recognition

89. Increasing terrorist threat—chemical warfare, water contamination, food contamination, bombing

90. Shift of green movement into mainstream

91. Rise in economic and political power of the China-India corridor

92. Increase in unemployment due to technology and open global market. Machines are replacing the need for some employees

93. Increase in use of the Internet as an entertainment vehicle

94. Increase in vegetarianism

95. Desire for fast and easy learning, "grazing" on learning, a quick route to becoming an expert in a particular subject

96. Desire for quick, easy-to-understand instructions

97. Desire for smart service in which the company knows the customer as an individual and knows their preferences

98. Wireless working—work anywhere, anytime

99. Youth raised on excitement. Desire for more entertainment in everything to combat the favorite expression "I'm bored"

APPENDIX E

List of Additional Criteria

In addition to the Six BIG-Picture criteria as discussed in Chapter 4 and Chapter 9, you and your team may wish to consider the following list of criteria for developing your own customized list.

It is important to note that your innovative idea may not meet these criteria, as many of these statements are related to maintaining efficiency within the organization. What is important, though, is that you consider these different statements in order to prepare your idea for presentation and for any opposition it may receive from those wanting to maintain the status quo.

(External Considerations) Our idea:

- Is simple enough that it can be understood
- Has strong in-market potential (revenue and share of market potential)

- Has the potential to grow rapidly
- Has long-term potential
- Has an identifiable target market
- Has a large enough identifiable target market
- Has multiple target groups
- Will have strong acceptance by customers or constituents
- Is needed or desired by the customer or constituents
- Provides differentiation from others in the marketplace
- Leads the market (is not another "me-too" initiative)
- Has little direct competition
- Has an acceptable window of opportunity before the competition follows
- Will create excitement
- Will make a difference in the marketplace
- Fits with the geographic market
- Avoids the need for price discounting

(Operational Considerations) Our idea:

- Is technically feasible
- Can be implemented
- Can be implemented easily
- Can be implemented in the short term (time to market considerations)
- Requires only a reasonable amount of resources to launch the innovation
- Requires only a reasonable amount of resources to sustain the innovation

- Has acceptable impact on other organizational initiatives
- Makes use of new technology
- Actually speeds up our processes or operations
- Represents a platform from which other initiatives can be launched
- Has a strong margin
- Has strong profit potential
- Can deliver profit potential that is greater than that of other initiatives
- Has a low cost of entry
- Has a low cost of expansion
- Leads to lower operating expenses
- Can be funded
- Takes advantage of our economies of scale
- Can be supported by our partners or suppliers
- Meets our legal and regulatory considerations

(Organizational Cultural Considerations) Our idea:

- Requires only a reasonable amount of human resources to launch the innovation
- Requires only a reasonable amount of human resources to sustain the innovation
- Has an acceptable impact on other organizational human resources and initiatives
- Has a reasonable chance of being accepted within this organization
- Can be managed

- Will not create significant adverse conditions that will be difficult to manage
- Will capture the interest of others so that they will want to adopt this idea
- Is consistent with the overall purpose of the organization
- Is consistent with the overall culture of the organization
- Will contribute to enhancing the overall image of the organization
- Will be good for the environment
- Uses our readily identifiable core competencies (within our organization or with partners)

Notes

Introduction

1. P. Evans and T. S. Wurster, *Blown to Bits* (Boston: Harvard Business School Press, 2000), p. 13.

2. PricewaterhouseCoopers, *1999 Global Growth and Innovation Study, Executive Summary,* (London, UK: PricewaterhouseCoopers, 1999), p. 6.

3. R. Jonash and T. Sommerlatte, *The Innovation Premium* (Reading, MA: Perseus, 1999), pp. 115, 119.

4. P. F. Drucker, *Management Challenges for the 21st Century* (New York: HarperCollins, 1999), p. 119.

Chapter 1

1. W. C. Miller, *Flash of Brilliance* (Reading, MA: Perseus, 1988).

2. D. Leonard and S. Straus, "Putting Your Company's Whole Brain to Work," *Harvard Business Review*, Reprint 97407 (1997): p.118.

3. H. Gardner, *Intelligences Reframed: Multiple Intelligences for the 21st Century.* (New York: Basic Books, 1999), pp. 41–43.

4. D. Goleman, P. Kaufman, and M. Ray, *The Creative Spirit* (New York: Penguin, 1992), p. 129.

5. R.Von Oech, *A Whack on the Side of the Head* (New York: Warner Books, 1998), p. 36.

6. Ibid., p. 30.

7. P. F. Drucker, "The Discipline of Innovation," *Harvard Business Review,* Reprint 98604 (November–December 1998): p. 6.

8. T. Kelley with J. Littman, *The Art of Innovation: Lessons in Creativity from IDEO, America's Leading Design Firm* (New York: Doubleday, 2001), p. 232.

Chapter 2

1. Drucker, "The Discipline of Innovation," p. 6.

2. R. Kreigel and D. Brandt, *Sacred Cows Make the Best Burgers* (New York: Warner Books, 1996), p. 1.

3. P. Senge, *The Fifth Discipline* (New York: Doubleday, 1994), p. 174.

4. A. Kingston, *The Edible Man* (Toronto: MacFarlane Walter Ross, 1994).

5. Kelley and Littman, p. 71.

Chapter 3

1. J. Rovin, "*I Wish I'd Thought of That!*" (Boca Raton, Fla.: Globe Communications, 1995), p. 15.

2. L. Koren, *283 Useful Ideas from Japan* (San Francisco: Chronicle Books, 1988), pp. 149 and 173.

3. Kelley and Littman, pp. 6 and 9.

4. B. Capodagli and L. Jackson, *The Disney Way: Harnessing the Management Secrets of Disney in Your Company* (New York: McGraw-Hill, 1999), p. 66.

5. G. Prince, *Group Planning and Problem Solving Methods in Engineering* (New York: Wiley, 1982), p. 360.

6. Capodagli and Jackson, p. 165.

7. M. Vance and D. Deacon, *Break Out of the Box* (Franklin Lakes, N.J.: Career Press, 1996), p. 91.

8. A. Osborn, *Applied Imagination: The Principles and Procedures of Creative Thinking* (New York: Scribner's, 1953).

9. Ibid.

Part 2: The Seeds of Strategic Thinking

1. Sun Tzu, *The Art of War*, trans. and ed. James Clavell (New York: Bantam Doubleday, 1983), p. 11.

Chapter 4

1. S. Haines, *Systems Thinking and Learning* (Amherst, Mass.: HRD Press, 1998), p. 6.

2. R. T. Pascale, M. Milleman, and L. Gioja, *Surfing on the Edge of Chaos* (New York: Crown, 2000), p. 8.

Chapter 5

1. Drucker, "The Discipline of Innovation," p. 3.

2. D. Leonard and J. Rayport, "Spark Innovation Through Empathic Design," *Harvard Business Review*, Reprint 97606 (1997): p. 110.

3. Ibid, p. 105.

4. E. von Hippel, "Lead Users: A Source of Novel Product Concepts," *Management Science* 32, no. 7 (July 1986): pp. 791–805.

5. M. L. Feldman and M. F. Spratt. *Five Frogs on a Log* (New York: HarperCollins, 1999), p. 29.

6. Rovin, p. 78.

7. S. Johnson, *Who Moved My Cheese?* (New York: Penguin Putnam, 1998), p. 68.

8. T. Levitt, "Marketing Myopia," *Harvard Business Review*, Reprint 75507 (September 1975).

9. Pascale, Milleman, and Gioja, p. 45.

10. W. Grulke, *10 Lessons from the Future* (London: Financial Times, Prentice Hall, 2001), p. 8.

11. Koren, p. 84.

Chapter 6

1. E. Rogers, *Diffusion of Innovations* (New York: Macmillan, 1962, 1971, 1983), p. 247.

2. D. Steinbock, *The Nokia Revolution* (New York: AMACOM, 2001), p.177.

3. C. M. Christensen, *The Innovator's Dilemma* (New York: HarperCollins, 1997), p. 116.

4. G. Hamel, *Leading the Revolution* (Boston: Harvard Business School Press, 2000), p. 11.

5. Koren, p. 120.

6. J. M. Higgins, *Innovate or Evaporate* (Winter Park, Fla.: New Management, 1995), p. 19.

7. Jonash and Sommerlatte, p. 26.
8. T. Peters, *The Circle of Innovation* (New York: Knopf, 1997), p. 191.
9. Steinbock, p. 283.
10. Steinbock, pp. 237, 238, 243.

Chapter 7

1. Senge, p. 22.
2. Goleman, Kaufman, and Ray, p. 129.
3. D. M. Amidon, *Innovation Strategy for the Knowledge Economy* (Boston: Butterworth-Heinemann, 1997), p. 16.
4. J. Kao, *Jamming* (New York: HarperCollins, 1996).

Chapter 8

1. S. Lundin, H. Paul, and J. Christensen, *Fish!* (New York: Hyperion, 2000).
2. D. Hock, *The Birth of the Chaordic Age* (San Francisco: Berrett-Koehler, 1999), p. 28.
3. I am indebted to my partner Alex Pattakos for these insights about Dr. Viktor Frankl's philosophy and work. Alex has, among other things, dedicated his own life to advancing the legacy of Dr. Frankl, who was his mentor and inspired him personally to bring logotherapy to the mainstream.
4. Capodagli and Jackson, p. 46.
5. Jonash and Sommerlatte, p. 108.
6. P. Chisholm, "Redesigning Work," *Maclean's*, v. 114, no. 10 (March 5, 2001): p. 35.

7. James Powell, innovation analyst with TELUS Mobility, personal interview with the author, July 2001.

8. Higgins, pp.109–111.

Chapter 9

1. Feldman and Spratt, p. 89.

2. S. Covey, *The 7 Habits of Highly Effective People: Powerful Lessons in Personal Change* (New York: Simon & Schuster, 1998).

3. Rogers, p. 165.

4. Kelley and Littman, p. 107.

5. Ibid., p. 106.

6. M. Schrage, *Serious Play: How the World's Best Companies Simulate to Innovate* (Boston: Harvard Business School Press, 1999), pp. 27–29.

7. Hamel, p. 193.

8. E. Schein, "How Can Organizations Learn Faster? The Challenge of Entering the Green Room," *Sloan Management Review* 34 (1993): 85–92.

9. R. McMath and T. Forbes, *What Were They Thinking?* (New York: Times Books, 1998), p. 31.

10. G. Pinchot, *Intrapreneuring* (New York: Harper & Row, 1985), p. 22.

11. M. Gladwell, *The Tipping Point* (London: Little, Brown, 2000), p. 4.

12. Ibid., p. 30.

13. H. Ebbinghaus, *Memory: A Contribution to Experimental Psychology* (New York: Dover, 1964), p. 76.

Chapter 10

1. Adrienne Clarkson, "The Speech from the Throne," address given in the Canadian Parliament in Ottawa, January 30, 2001.

2. Watson Wyatt Worldwide, *1999 Innovation Study and WorkSingapore Study* (Hong Kong and Singapore, 1999), p. 4.

3. C. Prather, *Blueprints for Innovation* (New York: American Management Association, 1995), p. 53.

4. Arthur Anderson, *1998 Innovation Best Practices Survey Report* (Chicago: Innovation Network and Arthur Anderson Global Best Practices, 1998), p. 4.

5. Koren, p. 148.

6. Hamel, p. 262.

7. R. Slater, *Jack Welch and the GE Way* (New York: McGraw-Hill, 1998), pp. 9, 118, 144.

8. R. Leifer, C. McDermott, G. O'Conner, L. Peters, M. Rice, and R. Veryzer, *Radical Innovation* (Boston: Harvard Business School Press, 2000), p. 30.

9. M. Cusumano, "How Microsoft Makes Large Teams Work Like Small Teams," *Sloan Management Review,* 39, no. 1 (Fall 1997), p. 1.

10. Higgins, p. 231.

11. Ibid., p. 211.

12. Ibid., p. 208.

13. A. Kohn, *Punished by Rewards* (New York: Houghton Mifflin, 1999), p. 68.

14. Schrage, p. 102.

15. Jonash and Sommerlatte, pp. 57 and 62.

Chapter 11

1. P. Jackson and H. Delehanty, *Sacred Hoops: Spiritual Lessons of a Hardwood Warrior* (New York: Hyperion, 1995), p. 9.

2. Drucker, *Management Challenges for the 21st Century*, p. 85.

3. Capodagli and Jackson, p. 11.

Recommended Reading List

Amidon, Debra M. *Innovation Strategy for the Knowledge Economy, The Ken Awakening*. Boston: Butterworth-Heinemann, 1997.

Arthur Andersen. *1998 Innovation Best Practices Survey Report.* Chicago: Innovation Network and Arthur Anderson Global Best Practices, 1998.

Buzan, Tony. *The Mind Map Book: How to Use Radiant Thinking to Maximize Your Brain's Untapped Potential.* New York: E.P. Dutton Publishing, 1996.

Capodagli, Bill and Lynn Jackson. *The Disney Way: Harnessing the Management Secrets of Disney in Your Company.* New York: McGraw-Hill, 1999.

Chisholm, P. "Redesigning Work," *Maclean's,* vol. 114, no. 10, (March 5, 2001): 35.

Christensen, Clayton M. *The Innovator's Dilemma.* New York: Harper-Collins, 1997.

Clarkson, Adrienne. "The Speech from the Throne." Address given in the Canadian Parliament, Ottawa, January 30, 2001.

Conference Board of Canada. *Building the Future: 1st Annual Innovation Report*. Ottawa, 1999.

Covey, Stephen R. *The 7 Habits of Highly Effective People: Powerful Lessons in Personal Change*. New York: Simon & Schuster, 1998.

Csikszentmihalyi, Mihaly. *Flow, The Psychology of Optimal Experience,* New York: HarperCollins, 1991.

Cusumano, M. "How Microsoft Makes Large Teams Work Like Small Teams." *Sloan Management Review,* Reprint 3911, vol. 39, no. 1, Fall 1997, pp. 1–15.

DeBono, Edward. *Serious Creativity, Using the Power of Lateral Thinking to Create New Ideas.* London: Little, Brown, 1993.

——— *Six Thinking Hats.* London: Little, Brown, 1999.

Drucker, Peter. F. *Management Challenges for the 21st Century*. New York: HarperCollins, 1999.

——— *Innovation and Entreprenuership.* New York: Harper & Row, 1985.

——— "The Discipline of Innovation." *Harvard Business Review,* Reprint 98604 (Nov.–Dec. 1998).

Dundon, Elaine, and Alex Pattakos. "Leading the Innovation Revolution: Will tht Real Spartacus Stand Up?" *The Journal for Quality and Particpation,* vol. 24, no. 4, Winter 2001, pp. 48–52.

Dundon, Elaine, and Alex Pattakos. *The Innovative Organization Assessment: A Holistic Approach.* King of Prussia, Pa.: Organization Design and Development Inc. HRDQ, 2000.

Ebbinghaus, Hermann. *Memory: A Contribution to Experimental Psychology*. Translated by Henry A. Ruger and Clara E. Bussenius. New York: Dover, 1964.

Evans, Philip, and Thomas S. Wurster. *Blown to Bits: How the New Economics of Information Transforms Strategy*. Boston: Harvard Business School Press, 2000.

Feldman, Mark L., and Michael F. Spratt. *Five Frogs on a Log: A CEO's Field Guide to Accelerating the Transition in Mergers, Acquisitions, and Gut Wrenching Change*. New York: HarperCollins, 1999.

Frankl, Viktor E. *Man's Search for Meaning*. Translated by Ilse Lasch. Boston: Beacon Press, 1959.

Frantz, R., and Alex Pattakos, eds. *Intuition at Work: Pathways to Unlimited Possibilities*. San Francisco: New Leaders Press, 1998.

Gardner, Howard. *Intelligences Reframed: Multiple Intelligences for the 21st Century*. New York: Basic Books, 1999.

Gladwell, Malcolm. *The Tipping Point: How Little Things Can Make a Big Difference*. London: Little, Brown, 2000.

Goldratt, Eliyahu M., and Jeff Cox. *The Goal: A Process of Ongoing Improvement*. Croton-on-Hudson, N.Y.: North River Press, 1984.

Goleman, Daniel, Paul Kaufman, and Michael Ray. *The Creative Spirit*. New York: Penguin, 1992.

Grulke, Wolfgang. *10 Lessons from the Future: Tomorrow Is a Matter of Choice. Make It Yours*. London: Financial Times Prentice Hall, 2001.

Gundling, Ernest. *The 3M Way to Innovation: Balancing People and Profit*. New York: Kodansha America Inc., 2000.

Haines, Stephen. *Systems Thinking and Learning*. Amherst, Mass.: HRD Press, 1998.

Hamel, Gary. *Leading the Revolution*. Boston: Harvard Business School Press, 2000.

Handy, Charles. *The Age of Paradox*. Boston: Harvard Business School Press, 1995.

Hermann, Ned. *The Creative Brain*. Lake Lure, N.C.: Ned Hermann Group, 1989.

Higgins, James M. *Innovate or Evaporate: Test and Improve Your Organization's Innovation Quotient*. Winter Park, Fla.: New Management, 1995.

Hirshberg, Jerry. *The Creative Priority: Driving Innovative Business in the Real World*. New York: HarperCollins, 1998.

Hock, Dee. *The Birth of the Chaordic Age*. San Francisco: Berrett-Koehler, 1999.

Houston, Jean. *Jump Time: Shaping Your Future in a World of Radical Change*. New York: Penguin Putnam, 2000.

Jackson, Phil, Hugh Delehanty, and Bill Bradley. *Sacred Hoops: Spiritual Lessons of a Hardwood Warrior.* New York: Hyperion, 1995.

Johnson, Spencer. *Who Moved My Cheese?An Amazing Way to Deal with Change in Your Work and in Your Life*. New York: Penguin Putnam, 1998.

Jonash, Ronald, and Tom Sommerlatte. *The Innovation Premium: How Next-Generation Companies Are Achieving Peak Performance and Profitability*. Reading, Mass.: Perseus, 1999.

Kao, John. *Jamming: The Art and Discipline of Business Creativity*. New York: HarperCollins, 1996.

Kelley, Tom, with Jonathan Littman. *The Art of Innovation: Lessons in Creativity from IDEO, America's Leading Design Firm*. New York: Doubleday, 2001.

Kingston, Anne. *The Edible Man.* Toronto: MacFarlane Walter Ross, 1994.

Kirton, Michael. "Adaptors and Innovators: A Description and Measure," *Journal of Applied Psychology*, vol. 17, no. 2, 1976, pp. 137–143.

Kohn, Alfie. *Punished by Rewards: The Problem with Gold Stars, Incentive Plans, A's, Praise, and Other Bribes.* New York: Houghton Mifflin, 1999.

Koren, Leonard. *283 Useful Ideas from Japan*. San Francisco: Chronicle Books, 1988.

Kreigel, Robert, and David Brandt. *Sacred Cows Make the Best Burgers*. New York: Warner Books, 1996.

Land, George, and Beth Jarman. *Breakpoint and Beyond: Mastering the Future Today*. New York: Harper Collins, 1992.

Leifer, Richard, Christopher McDermott, Gina O'Conner, Lois Peters, Mark Rice, and Robert Veryzer. *Radical Innovation*. Boston: Harvard Business School Press, 2000.

Leonard, Dorothy, and J. Rayport. "Spark Innovation Through Empathic Design," *Harvard Business Review,* Reprint 97606, November–December 1997, pp. 102–113.

Leonard, Dorothy, and S. Strauss. "Putting Your Company's Whole Brain to Work," *Harvard Business Review,* Reprint 97407, July–August 1997, pp. 111–121.

Leonard, Dorothy, and Walter Swap. *When Sparks Fly: Igniting Creativity in Groups*. Boston: Harvard Business School Press, 1999.

Levitt, Ted. "Marketing Myopia," *Harvard Business Review,* Reprint 75507, September–October 1975, pp. 1–13.

Lewin, Roger. *Complexity: Life at the Edge of Chaos*. 2nd Edition. Chicago: University of Chicago Press, 1999.

Lundin, Stephen, Harry Paul, and John Christensen. *Fish! A Remarkable Way to Boost Morale and Improve Results*. New York: Hyperion, 2000.

McGartland, Grace. *Thunderbolt Thinking: Transform Your Insights and Options Into Powerful Business Results*. Toronto: Stoddart, 1994.

McMath, Robert, and Thom Forbes. *What Were They Thinking?* New York: Times Books, 1998.

McNeilly, Mark. *Sun Tzu and the Art of Business: Six Strategic Principles for Managers*. New York: Oxford University Press, 1996.

Marrow, Alfred F. *The Practical Theorist: The Life and Work of Kurt Lewin*. New York: Basic Books, 1969.

Messer, Mari. *Pencil Drawings: New Ways to Free Your Creative Spirit.* Cincinnati: Walking Stick Press, 2001.

Miller, William C. *The Creative Edge: Fostering Innovation Where You Work.* Reading, Mass.: Addison-Wesley, 1987.

——— *Flash of Brilliance: Inspiring Creativity Where You Work.* Reading, Mass.: Perseus, 1988.

Mintzberg, Henry. *The Rise and Fall of Strategic Planning.* New York: Free Press, 1994.

Osborn, Alex. *Applied Imagination: The Principles and Procedures of Creative Thinking.* New York: Scribner's, 1953.

Pascale, Richard T., Mark Milleman, and Linda Gioja. *Surfing on the Edge of Chaos.* New York: Crown, 2000.

Peters, Tom. *Reinventing Work: The Brand You.* New York: Knopf, 2001.

——— *The Circle of Innovation.* New York: Knopf, 1997.

——— *The Pursuit of Wow.* New York: Vintage, 1994.

Peters, Tom, and Robert Waterman, Jr. *In Search of Excellence: Lessons from America's Best-Run Companies.* New York: Warner Books, 1982.

Pinchot, Gifford. *Intrapreneuring: Why You Don't Have to Leave the Corporation to Become an Entrepreneur.* New York: Harper & Row, 1985.

Pink, Daniel. *Free Agent Nation: How America's New Independent Workers Are Transforming the Way We Live.* New York: Warner Books, 2001.

Prather, Charles, and Lisa Gundry. *Blueprints for Innovation: How Creative Processes Can Make You and Your Company More Competitive.* New York: American Management Association, 1995.

PricewaterhouseCoopers. *1999 Global Growth and Innovation Study.* London: PricewaterhouseCoopers, 1999.

Prince, George. *Group Planning and Problem Solving Methods in Engineering.* New York: Wiley, 1982.

Quinn, James Brian, Jordan Baruch, and Karen Anne Zien. *Innovation Explosion: Using Intellect and Software to Revolutionize Growth Strategies*. New York: Simon & Schuster, 1997.

Ray, Michael, and Rochelle Myers. *Creativity in Business.* New York: Doubleday, 1989.

Ries, Al, and Jack Trout. *Positioning: The Battle for Your Mind.* New York: McGraw-Hill, 2001.

Robinson, Alan, and Stan Stern. *Corporate Creativity: How Innovation and Improvement Actually Happen.* San Francisco: Berrett-Koehler, 1998.

Rogers, Everett. *Diffusion of Innovations*. New York: Macmillan, 1983.

Rovin, Jeff. "*I Wish I'd Thought of That!*" Boca Raton, Fla.: Globe Communications, 1995.

Schein, E. "How Can Organizations Learn Faster? The Challenge of Entering the Green Room," *Sloan Management Review,* 34 (1993): pp. 85–92.

Schrage, Michael. *Serious Play: How the World's Best Companies Simulate to Innovate*. Boston: Harvard Business School Press, 1999.

Senge, Peter. *The Fifth Discipline: The Art and Practice of the Learning Organization*. New York: Doubleday, 1994.

Singapore 21 Committee. *Singapore 21*. Singapore: Prime Minister's Office, 1999.

Slater, Robert. *Get Better or Get Beaten: 29 Leadership Secrets from GE's Jack Welch.* New York: McGraw-Hill, 2001.

——— *Jack Welch and the GE Way: Management Insights and Leadership Secrets of the Legendary CEO*. New York: McGraw-Hill, 1998.

Steinbock, Dan. *The Nokia Revolution: The Story of an Extraordinary Company That Transformed an Industry*. New York: AMACOM, 2001.

Sun Tzu, *The Art of War*. Translated and edited by James Clavell. New York: Bantam Doubleday, 1983.

Thorpe, Scott. *How to Think Like Einstein*. Naperville, Ill.: Sourcebooks, 2000.

Tushman, Michael, and Charles O'Reilly. *Winning Through Innovation: A Practical Guide to Leading Organization Change and Renewal.* Boston: Harvard Business School Press, 1996.

Vaill, Peter. *Managing as a Performing Art: New Ideas for a World of Chaotic Change*. San Francisco: Jossey-Bass, 1989.

Vance, Mike, and Diane Deacon. *Break Out of the Box*. Franklin Lakes, N.J.: Career Press, 1996.

Von Hippel, Eric. "Lead Users: A Source of Novel Product Concepts," *Management Science* 32, no. 7 (July 1986): pp. 791–805.

Von Oech, Roger. *A Whack on the Side of the Head*. New York: Warner Books, 1998.

Watson Wyatt Worldwide. "1999 Innovation Study and Work Singapore Study." Singapore: Watson Wyatt, 1999.

Wheatley, Margaret J. *Leadership and the New Science: Discovering Order in a Chaotic World*. San Francisco: Berrett-Koehler, 1999.

Wycoff, Joyce. *Mindmapping: Your Personal Guide to Exploring Creativity and Problem-Solving*. New York: Berkley, 1991.

Index

About the Author

Elaine Dundon, MBA, is the founder and chief strategist of The Innovation Group Consulting, an international firm dedicated to elevating the innovative thinking potential of individuals, teams, and organizations. She is a highly regarded keynote speaker, trainer, consultant, and thought leader in the field of Innovation Management and also designed and taught a "first of its kind" course on Innovation Management in the business program at the University of Toronto. Elaine resides in Santa Fe, New Mexico, USA, and Toronto, Ontario, Canada, and can be reached at elaine@innovationguru.com